NORTH COUNTRY NOTEBOOK

Also by George Vukelich

Fisherman's Beach
North Country Notebook (Volume 1)

NORTH COUNTRY NOTEBOOK
Volume 2
George Vukelich
Illustrations by Dan Metz

North Country Press
Madison, Wisconsin

First edition, first printing, 1992
Copyright © by George Vukelich

North Country Press
3934 Plymouth Circle
Madison, Wisconsin 53705

Cover and jacket design by Thill Design, Middleton, Wisconsin

Printed in the United States of America

Library of Congress Cataloging-in-Publication Data

Vukelich, George.
    North country notebook / George Vukelich.—1st ed.
      p.   cm.
    ISBN 0-944133-09-6 (cloth: v.2): $17.95. — ISBN 0-944133-10-X
    (paper): $10.95
        1. Upper Peninsula (Mich.)—Social life and customs. 2. Fishing-
    Michigan—Upper Peninsula. 1. Title.
    F572.N8V84   1992
    977.4'9—dc20   92-25131
                                                              CIP

for Helen Louise
who continues to make our journey
A Real Trip

Contents

NORTH COUNTRY NOTEBOOK

GREETINGS

I'm your new neighbor and I thought I'd better introduce myself right off so you could see for yourself that I ought to fit in pretty well here and to allay your fears that this neck of the woods is going to hell in a handbasket.

I've been potsing around in the Wisconsin woods all my life, and after the Seven-Foot Nun taught me how to use a pencil I started writing about those woods. After she taught me how to sharpen the pencil, there was no holding me.

I got a lot of my love for the Wisconsin boonies from my Old Man who said that the North Country here reminded him of his native Yugoslavia and that was a big reason he and my mother bought a little oldtimey resort with housekeeping cabins on Big Stone Lake across from Carl Marty's old Showboat and Northernaire in the mid 1940s. The Old Man died 14 years ago and is buried in Three Lakes. My mother ran the resort until she died this spring at 80. She's right at his side again and that's fitting because that's the way they went through life.

The Old Man taught me how to fish and how to hunt and some of his lessons are unforgettable and God knows I've tried to forget them.

There was the first time he took me squirrel hunting in a Waukesha County oak woods, and when he left me alone I fired off my .22 into a squirrel's nest. When he came back and found out what I'd done, he just calmly took the rifle away from me, unloaded it, and literally wrapped it around a tree, saying that I was too damn dumb to go hunting just yet.

This was the same man who, because he couldn't write English, would have my mother write a note to the Seven-Foot Nun, who ran Holy Assumption grade school the way Patton would later run Third Army, saying: "Please excuse George from school. He is going fishing with his father." Then off we would go in the cold Wisconsin springtime to fish the walleye run at New London, Fremont, and the Shiocton flats.

I also got a lot of love for the Wisconsin boonies from Gordon MacQuarrie and Mel Ellis, who were writing about the great outdoors for the *Milwaukee Journal* in those days. They

1

were probably the finest outdoor writers in this hemisphere, and to think they were on the SAME paper at the SAME time is, as Steady Eddy used to say down at the baitshop, just plain unthinkable.

I got to interview Mel Ellis at Little Lakes back in 1971 and I put that right in the same class as the interviews we did with Frank Lloyd Wright at Spring Green, Sigurd Olson at Ely, Minnesota, and John D. Voelker at his beloved brookie-filled Frenchman's Pond in the Upper Peninsula.

I found out that day at Little Lakes why Mel Ellis was a great outdoor writer. It was because he was a great perceptive Being.

"I don't think we treated nature right when I was a boy," Mel said. "I don't think we had any concept of how to treat nature. Today we know a lot more about how to treat nature than we did then. When the Horicon Marsh was going in, only a handful of people fought for it. Today you could get thousands and thousands to back a project like that."

I asked Mel if he believed in God.

"I cannot but believe," he said, "that there is a governing force. The universe is too vast, too well regulated, and too handily put together not to have something guiding it. I have experienced nature as a deep, deep, significant feeling that I'm part of the earth. An owl at night or a coyote howling or a bright running stream are all part of me and I am part of them. We're all part of each other."

When it came to his profession of writing, Mel is one of three people in this life who gave me any worthwhile advice on how to do it. Mari Sandoz and August Derleth were the other two. They both said: "Go home and WRITE!" Mel took the advice one bootstep further. He said writing should "say something" to the reader.

"If you haven't got something to say," Mel said, "what the hell are you writing for? I think that everything you write should say something. I think you should try to teach as you go along, but in an offhand way. The teaching should be incidental to a good story. I think you should show some side of life, good or bad, and let the reader do his own moralizing and draw his own conclusion."

North Country Notebook has been through a lot of changes, a lot of incarnations, since it first started in the old *Wisconsin*

Tales and Trails magazine back in the pleistocene. There's even an audio version carried around the state over Wisconsin Public Radio on Sunday nights.

But it's what it started out to be—a lifelong pilgrimage along those blazed trails in the bush. My Old Man and Gordon MacQuarrie and Mel Ellis left some pretty big boot tracks in these parts and I like to think we're just following along, and taking time to smell the flowers while we do the fillets. Hope you think so, too.

SPRING

Solid as a Rock

We were on a canoe trip for brook trout down a lovely
stream in the Albany River country north of Nakina,
Ontario. The twin Beechcraft with one canoe slung between
its floats had dropped us into the small lake out of which the
trout stream flowed. On its banks we found an aluminum canoe
that had been cached there under the branches of a pine tree.
There would be five of us in the two canoes.

The pilot reminded us to have the Hudson's Bay store
manager radio him when we got downriver to Ogoki Post and
he would pick us up there when we were ready. Then he taxied
across the little lake and took off.

When we turned over the cached canoe we found a nice
little hole in its flank. At first glance, it was easy to think that
somebody had put a bullet through it, but then Bob Resch
studied it and he said it was a "rub hole." When you studied
it, you could see that Resch was right.

Somehow the canoe had slipped partways off the bank and
had just rubbed up against a tree trunk, back and forth, up and
down, and presto! You had a rub hole. It could have happened
when the ice went out last spring. Highwater. Too much play

5

in the chain. We never did find out how long the canoe had been cached there by the fly-in people.

Resch got a tube of liquid aluminum out of his pack and patched the hole. Only Resch would have liquid aluminum in his pack. The rest of us had Band-Aids and a few rolls of adhesive tape. We loaded the two canoes, paddled across the lake and entered "the stream of dreams."

The river was low, the traditional "rock garden" through which we dragged the canoes from one floatable, fishable pool to another. But in those floatable, fishable pools the river gave us brook trout, wild Canadian brook trout that ran four, five, and six pounds! The trout looked as big and beautiful as salmon in their flaming colors. The trout fought like salmon too. Deep plunging runs that got your heart pounding and your gear screeching.

I remembered the brook trout in the little Wisconsin creeks. They now seemed like herring, like sardines.

Brook trout this size used to live in Wisconsin too. The old explorers of the Bois Brule noted in their journals that they broke through a hundred beaver ponds from the mouth at Lake Superior up to the point where the bridge now carries Highway 2 across the dark river.

An Army lieutenant in the 1800s noted in his journals that his men caught hundreds of trout, finally quitting not because the fish stopped biting, but because the men became arm-weary and tired.

My God. Can you imagine trout fishing like that?

"You hate to say that the trout fishing was better in the Olden Days," Steady Eddy says, "but let me say only that the trout fishing was better in the Olden Days." In our beloved Wisconsin, you have only to read the histories of the early settlers at Green Bay, for instance. There are accounts of lake trout—some of them weighing a hundred pounds—stacked like cordwood on the beaches.

One morning on the river, our guide, Sandy, took everyone except me downriver to some feeder creeks that he said ran cold as glacier melt, and "really big trout" put their noses right there. Big brookies were always stacked up there like cordwood, he said.

I didn't go, not because I was arm-weary from the previous days. It was just that this was a chance to be alone and hang out with the river.

There is something about a wilderness camp in the clean midmorning of a sunny Canadian day—cleaning up is not a chore! I fed the woodfire all the paper and cardboard scraps from breakfast, washed and boiled the cups, cutlery and mess kits and put everything on a rock to dry. Then I got fresh water from the river for tea. While I waited for the water to boil, I unzipped the sleeping bags and spread them over the huge granite outcroppings to air and dry the damp out of them. I moved all the packs into the full sunlight too.

When the water boiled, I made tea and took my cup to the sloping outcropping of Canadian Shield and hunkered down until the hot stone toasted my buns. The sun felt good on my back. Its warmth came right through the damp wool shirt.

The sun felt good and I felt good. I also felt very sorry for my friends who were missing all this goodness because they were downriver fishing this morning away and catching all those monstrous brook trout.

I sipped my tea. The river gurgled and flashed past into the rock garden. The stillness was like church.

Then I got that spooky feeling you get when you know something is watching you. Here I was, miles from any human. We hadn't seen anyone on this river. We were probably the only people on it. I figured it must be an animal watching.

I panned the whole scene, left to right, slowly, very s-l-o-w-l-y, looking, as the Indians say, with "soft eyes." I did it twice, three times. Four times. There was nothing that I could see watching me. But I knew *something* was watching me. My eyes were drawn—pulled—to a huge rock sitting in the river near the far shore. Even at high water, that rock would never be submerged. It came to me that the rock was here thousands of years before I was born and would be here thousands of years after I was dead. It also came to me that the rock was watching me. It had to be. It was as though I had locked onto another pair of eyes.

I didn't feel fear, that is to say, I didn't feel that the rock was malevolent or evil or anything like that. I felt: Of course.

I said: "Thank you." Out loud. I never told the others because they were always talking about the trout.

Shaman's Lake

This poem is a *sestina*, an old French form that employs 36 stanzas of six lines each to produce the illusion of rhyming.

The *sestina* is also a narrative form of poetry that was traditionally used to tell of heroic, larger-than-life happenings. As Steady Eddy points out, the form is sometimes utilized at the American Legion Bar in Three Lakes when the going gets tough and the tough play cribbage.

A shaman, as you know, is a medicine man or a medicine woman with great powers that seem downright inexplicable, unexplainable. When you meet a shaman, you'll know you've met one. Then again, maybe not.

When the war was over, we came back home
for only one brief winter, then the following spring
we quit the city, packed up, went north like geese.
Beyond the end of the gravel road, we paddled for days.
Then for one week. Then for two. Then for four.
We stopped only when we found this lake.

That year we never knew this was the shaman's lake.
Before next ice-out he came, camped in his ancestral home.
Looking right through us, he built his fire, faced all four
directions. Murmuring in the last snow before spring.
In three days' time, ice was tinkling. The following days
filled to the brim with the bugling of geese.

Those mornings we woke to thousands of geese,
no, tens of thousands, filling the sky, filling the lake.
It went on like that for days and days and days,
yet always we sensed that this was not their home.
That spring on this lake was like no other spring,
the strangest season of any of the four.

It seemed the great flocks were coming from all four
corners of the world. Great clouds of the wildest geese.

Blues and Snows and Canadas, babbling torrents of spring
rushing down, raising up the waters of the lake. We
watched the Old Man watching geese rain down on his home.
He never moved, not a step, for three nights and three days.

He seemed in a trance, the geese fell quiet those days.
Tens of thousands of geese, still as gravestones at four
in the morning. Finally, they moved, seeming to home
on the silent figure of the Old Man. Surrounded by geese
he disappeared from our glasses as every goose left the lake
empty. *Every* goose climbing the far shore that eerie spring.

We have told some others of those happenings that spring,
those happenings that yet disturb our nights and our days.
When the geese round the Old Man moved back to the lake,
there was no human to be seen on that shore! There were four
stones, marking, we think, East, West, South, North. The geese
then flew north, forsaking, forever, this lake we call home.

Once, the northern spring was our favorite of the four.
Now, the lake ice goes out and there are no geese.
Not a one, in this Godforsaken place we call home.

We think of them often as we walk the far shore,
of the geese and the shaman gone to only God knows where.
Night after starry night when the chill darkness falls,
we stay inside the cabin, dreaming at our fire,
seeing in the stove flames, the Old Man's face
and the birds gathered round him, silent as stones.

We *know* what we saw in this strange place of stones.
A mystery happened out there on that shore.
Mystery, so near, yet as far from our world as the face
of the moon, for when we walk that far shore where
the Old Man stood, there comes a crackling of fire.
We see it: Blue, Green, *electric* fire. It surges, falls.

It is a mark of Holy Places, of mountains, of waterfalls,
of crystal pure waters rushing, rushing through stones.
Once, twice, in sunlight we tried to light our cooking fire
in the exact place the Old Man had built his on that shore.
Our woodsticks, brittle, bone dry, *would not burn* where
the shaman's old fires still blacken the granite rock face.

9

We do not know how you would put the proper face
on factual happenings such as these. There are pitfalls
in just telling this story. We have to be careful where
we tell it. Some people get angry enough to throw stones
at you. They think all that stuff about the crazy far shore
is only to make them look foolish. It sets them on fire.

But whether people stay cool as ice or get hot as fire
makes about as much difference as a flea on the face
of a glacier. What happened on that far, mysterious shore
happened. On this planet, we think everything falls,
pulled by gravity, toward the center, but there are stones
subject to a different law and a shaman can tell you where.

We think we know why the shaman left us, but where
he went we do not know. He left because we came. A fire
on the beach and then he left us with stones.
That was frightening enough, but today we have seen his face
in three places: Once, a radiance in the waterfalls.
A luminescence above the lake. Watching, from the far shore.

Now, another terrifying knowledge stares right in our face.
We are at the edge of sheer terror, the edge of the falls.
No dry woodsticks will burn now on either lake shore.

The Spirit Endures

In the chill of the spring morning, the old German short-
haired pointer stood next to Charlie Bradley like a sculp-
ture in the thin sunlight.

Only her nostrils were moving. You wanted to throw your
down vest over her knobby flanks. You wanted to carry her
inside to the warm, sweet spot next to the stove.

"Old dogs in the nippy mornings," Steady Eddy says, "remind me of old ballplayers. They know they can still do it and
you know they can still do it. Only it takes a while for the old
bones to get warmed up enough so they want to do it."

"Flick is going to be thirteen years old," Charlie said.
"She was a present to us from Nina's sister."

Nina is Charlie's wife. Nina is also the daughter of the late, great Aldo Leopold, whose book *A Sand County Almanac* has become the bible of the environmental movement. Leopold's converted chicken coop, "the shack," has become a shrine of the environmental movement. Nina and Charlie live on the old Leopold farmstead, only a short hike from the world-famous "shack." As long as they can remember, Leopold dogs have always prowled this storied piece of Wisconsin River sand country.

"Aldo loved dogs," Charlie says, "especially hunting dogs. There was always at least one around the place. 'Flick' was the name that Aldo always gave his dogs if they were female. If the dog was a male, Aldo called it 'Gus.' "

Charlie Bradley patted Flick's bony flanks.

"Of course," he said, "Flick isn't the hunter she once was. I first saw the cloudiness in her lenses about three years ago. Now, she's blind and pretty deaf, too. I think she can hear a shrill whistle, but that's about it. She hardly hears me at all."

Flick One. Flick Two. Flick Three. How many Flicks have there been? How many? Kicking up rabbits and flushing grouse and even jumping deer, probably doing that just for the sheer hell of it because those big spooky deer were probably scared witless by those little demon stalkers.

You look at old Flick and you can sense the excitement that once was: The hunter's legs pumping through the marshland, the joy of mud and marsh and exploding water and then some wild thing up and running for its life with this great, bolting fire-eyed fury hot on the trail—too smart and too strong to be fooled for long.

Old Flick was a shadow of that now but you could still see it if you looked hard enough, the way you can see the beauty in Grandma's face if you *really* looked.

The German short-haired pointer was bred for the hunt. Beneath that civilized veneer was the same wildness that lived in the quarry she had pursued all her life. Now, grown old, her legs unable to pump anymore, she stood shivering in the Wisconsin spring the very way we will all come to stand. Waiting. Waiting.

"Still, she's better than she used to be," Charlie said. "Remember the winter of 1981? Heavy snows, but we also had

11

a rain that winter that put a crust on everything. We used to see blood on the snow where deer broke through and cut themselves up. The crust was like glass, broken glass.

"Well, Flick broke through, too, and she broke a toe. Had all kinds of trouble with it. She wasn't her old self. We finally had it amputated. It took her about two or three weeks to get over the operation and that seemed to bring her back to life—she was almost her old self. Just when she seemed about ready to cave in, the operation gave her a new lease on life.

"She can't hear and she can't see but she still has that hunter's nose. She can still smell the action."

Charlie says Flick wakes up pretty sluggish these days and stays sluggish most of the day. She sparks up if they're going to walk the trails of the Leopold Reserve, but she seems also to know when they're only walking out to the mailbox and she skips that, thank you.

We were going to walk the trails this day and Flick bestirred herself and dragged herself along.

Within ten minutes, she was coursing along like Snoopy, nose to the grindstone, tending to business. Within twenty minutes, she was trotting ahead of us, her progress marked by sentinel jays. Within the hour, she was out of sight, more than in, the sun and the old rhythms of the hunt stirring the coals of the primeval fires.

When Flick finally heaved back into sight, her appearance startled us. She moved like a younger animal—strong, lethal, almost flowing. Her step was firm, her body rippling. Her teeth were clenched like a steel trap—*on a struggling possum.*

I don't know if she knew exactly where we were, because she did a thing then that dogs usually do in secret. Still clutching the dying possum, Flick dug away the duff and dirt at the base of a tree. Then, she bit down HARD on the possum's neck and back and the possum died. Flick proceeded to stuff the possum's body into the fresh hole. Then, using her muzzle as a shovel, she covered the corpse. It was very efficient. It was also very impressive.

She trotted right past us, her carriage high, her tail high, her demeanor almost arrogant, haughty. *Don't count this old dog out yet* her body language seemed to be saying. Then, she was off and away down the trail that leads to the shack that Aldo Leopold left to his family, which includes all of us.

Only the Crane Remains

S itting in the Leopold Pines during a Wisconsin spring is akin to sitting in the Leopold "shack" in his beloved Sand County in the Wisconsin River bottomlands.

There is that residual chill in the air, the sense that the glacial ice retreated only yesterday and that if you poked into the pine needle carpet with a bare finger you would scratch into permafrost.

It is this moment of spring that Aldo Leopold captured for us in the live trap of *A Sand County Almanac.*

The winter lands, the winter waters are unlocked. Common loons are fishing in Wingra. Whooping cranes are northbound on their annual spring flight from Texas to the Canadian Northwest Territories. And the sandhill cranes are back in Aldo Leopold country.

"Of all the things in *A Sand County Almanac,*" Nina Leopold Bradley says, "the piece about the sandhill cranes, 'Marshland Elegy,' is probably the family's favorite of all our father's writings."

You can close your eyes any morning in the Wisconsin spring, and no matter where you are, if you listen hard enough, you can hear the sandhill cranes muttering around in the marsh. You can hear Aldo Leopold, muttering to himself, as he puts it all down on paper.

❈ ❈ ❈

A dawn wind stirs on the great marsh. With almost imperceptible slowness it rolls a bank of fog across the wide morass. Like the white ghost of a glacier the mists advance, riding over phalanxes of tamarack, sliding across the bog meadows heavy with dew. A single silence hangs from horizon to horizon.

"Out of some far recess of the sky, a tinkling of little bells falls soft upon the listening land. Then again silence. Now comes a baying of some sweet-throated hound, soon the clamor of a responding pack. Then a clear blast of hunting horns, out of the sky into the fog.

"High horns, low horns, silence, and finally a pandemonium of trumpets, rattles, croaks, and cries that almost shakes

13

the bog with its nearness, but without yet disclosing whence it comes. At last a glint of sun reveals the approach of a great echelon of birds. On motionless wings they emerge from the lifting mists, sweep a final arc of sky, and settle in clamorous descending spirals to their feeding grounds. A new day has begun on the crane marsh."

✻ ✻ ✻

"Birds have no boundaries," ornithologist George Archibald is fond of saying up at the International Crane Foundation. "They have a lot to teach us."

Our appreciation of the cranes, Aldo Leopold pointed out, grows with the slow unraveling of earthly history. The crane's tribe, we now know, stems out of the remote Eocene, when, as Steady Eddy likes to proclaim: "The strange birds in the skies outnumbered the strange birds on the freeways."

The crane's contemporaries from that ancient time have long since waddled into the tar pits of extinction, their very voices bulk-erased by an unsentimental Nature not given to saving every flower that bloomed or every bloodline that flowered.

In some primal swamp, the crane was just another pretty voice in the crowd. Now the crane is the only voice left. The crowd is gone, transformed, the molecules of the millennia flowing into our gas tanks, the mindless gurgling only a memory of titanic sounds that once dominated this planet.

Yet the crane speaks now as the crane spoke then.

The crane keeps the faith and the marshlands keep the crane. The crane, Aldo wrote in wonderment, is the symbol of our untamable past, of that incredible sweep of millennia that underlies and conditions the daily affairs of birds and humankind.

"Their annual return," Aldo noted, "is the ticking of the geologic clock. Upon the place of their return, they confer a peculiar distinction. Amid the endless mediocrity of the commonplace, a crane marsh holds a paleontological patent of nobility, won in the march of aeons and revocable only by shotgun."

I open my eyes and I don't see cranes anymore. But I still hear them, muttering, out of sight, in the marsh. There is a pterodactyl in there with them.

If you can't get away to the North Country as often as you would like, the next best thing may be getting away to the Leopold Pines in the University of Wisconsin Arboretum.

The moment you enter the special hush that pine forests exude—I used to think it was like being in church, but Steady Eddy says it's also like being a paratrooper as your plane approaches the Drop Zone—you're in the Nicolet National Forest, and Lake Julia lies just beyond the next rise.

It's the silence, of course.

It can be spooky.

You don't get that kind of silence out on the open prairie. The sky is too high. There are no trees to cast shadows. The wind can sweep through, unfettered, and the seas of grass can be as noisy and gurgling as waves rolling into the shallows.

When you enter the Leopold Pines, you are behind the sea wall.

You are in the cathedral and the wind is a gentle murmur, high up in the dark, living dome.

❁ ❁ ❁

Aldo, Aldo
These pines are called after you.
They are a sanctuary, these precious few.
There is talk of the freeway coming through.

Dark Side of the Loon

Folks up in Eagle River could forgive Nick Van Der Puy for being a professional guide with a bachelor's degree from Ripon College. They could even forgive the fact that his degree is in philosophy. But what some folks consider unforgivable is that Nick, a non-Indian, sides with the Indians in the ongoing dispute over Chippewa treaty rights.

Nick writes letters to the paper, speaks out for the Indians in the Eagle River Guides Association meetings ("We have 21 members and *none* thinks like I do on this") and goes on Indian sweat lodges. Prior to this spearing season, he organized a weekend of seminars in Minocqua-Woodruff supporting the

15

Chippewa. That prompted an anonymous phone call warning he was going to get "a spear in the head."

"I have trouble in town," Nick admitted when we talked on the phone the other day, "and it's gotten worse since this spearing season. I was out guiding with a customer last week and I had my brother and my four-year-old son, Jake, along. A little MG sped past us and somebody yelled out: 'Fuck you, Nick!'

"Yesterday I walked out of the bank and there was a pickup truck passing by with an antitreaty woman in it. I could just make out her lips and she was saying: 'Asshole!' I resisted an impulse to follow her. I figured: Be cool. Walk peacefully. But speak your onions."

Nick, who has been a full-time professional guide since 1979—the same year he married Nan Susan Andrew—speaks his onions about the "ugly mood" in town.

"Last night," he says, "I read Shirley Jackson's *The Lottery* just to try to understand how a community can get mad, and I think that's what's happened up here. They reinforce their hatred and their ignorance. They elect 'their own' D.A., judge, sheriff, school board members, and they remain insulated from the outside."

Nick thinks that people in positions of power—the elected civic officials, business leaders, clergy, educators, social workers—are silent on the subject of racism in the North because their own standing stems from a system that's forced dominance over Native Americans.

"The local sheriff spoke out, though," Nick says. "Jim Williquette. I think he exercised very poor judgment. He went on local radio and said that he wished he wasn't sheriff so he could go out and 'protest at the landings.' Like most of the antitreaty people, the facts are lost on him. No matter how thoroughly and carefully you explain the basis of treaty rights to him, the man is unmoved. I think it's because he wants to return to the status quo of white dominance. He does not want to share power.

"Now, having said that about the sheriff, let me say that the coppers put up with a lot of grief at the landings, and by 'coppers' I mean the sheriff's deputies, the police, the DNR wardens, all the security people. They were pelted with 'wrist-

16

rocket' slingshots. They took a pretty good beating. . . . Despite their own feelings about treaty rights, they did their job."

Nick feels that the anti-Indian position up north originates in an anticivil rights backlash and has nothing to do with "equal justice for all." He speculates that if the spearing stopped tomorrow and the tribes sold out their rights, the north would have "an open season for wholesale Cape Cod-style development," and the local people would wind up working in a 7-Eleven store making minimum wage.

He argues that there's a tremendous demand in Eagle River for part-time help, because employers don't want to pay workmen's compensation and insurance.

"There's a continual erosion in the standard of living up here for everybody, including whites. That economic reality has been deflected into an anti-Indian position by the leaders of the antitreaty movement.

"The average income in Oneida County is well below the poverty level and not just for Indians, for non-Indians too. This is a Third World peripheral colony! You have to look at it in those terms. There are economic forces here. Cheap labor. Lakeshore development destroying the environment."

Nick thinks the white business community should invite Indians in because Indians bring authenticity. He says most of his customers—"professional people from Chicago, Madison and Milwaukee"—are interested in Ojibway culture, going to Flambeau and "getting genuine moccasins."

"They've looked in Eagle River," he laughs, "and they find moccasins made in Minnesota and beads made in China. I think a genuine Indian crafts store would do well and would help the economy too. Like Katy's in Madison.

"One afternoon I was driving on County J between Minocqua-Woodruff and St. Germain, going to check out Carrol Lake, and I got behind a vehicle with some kids in it, young males 18 to 24 years old. They were swerving and it looked like they'd been drinking. Then I saw a porcupine ahead, waddling across the road. The kids swerved to hit it! They went way into the ditch and did hit it. The porcupine just flushed its quills. Quills were everywhere. The kids never stopped. I was going to stop to see how the porcupine was doing, but it was waddling into the forest and it just kept going.

"That's when I realized everything is going to work out up here."

FROGGING AROUND

Frogging Around

A t first blush, nothing has changed on the little North Country lake. The ancient planks of the wooden pier still remind you of silvery "distressed" barn boards. The thin reeds still stick up out of the clear, clean shallows like swizzle sticks. Greenie frogs still scatter ahead of you as you walk the shore. They cascade into the water like lemmings.

To stand in this place where you have stood so often before is to slip once more through that seam in Time and reenter the reality that is as hard to reenter as childhood.

This is still an Unspoiled Place. There is still Magic here. It touches you with the vibrations of dragonfly wings and the perfume of sun-warmed balsam, fragrant as joss sticks burning before the Buddha. Often I have confessed to Steady Eddy that just sitting here is like going to church.

"Well," Steady Eddy has often confessed to me, "it's like going to church and just sitting there—in your canoe."

True. On this unspoiled, magical North Country lake, one of the great joys that grownup people have is to sit here on beautiful Bluegill Bay and be little kids again.

You wear cutoff jeans. You fish with a flyrod and poppers. You fill up the plastic pail with bluegills until the poppers unravel and your tangled city ways do likewise.

It is something indeed to be in a place where the only sounds you hear for hours on end—*"Your end,"* Steady Eddy

21

notes—is the *slurp, slurp, slurp* of the peewee poppers being inhaled, snorted down, by very pugnacious bluegills.

The kind of silence you find here in Bluegill Bay is not to be found in the cities.

This is the silence that mends the body and heals the soul. With deep quiet comes deep peace and the tranquility that Sigurd Olson up in the Boundary Waters used to say "was beyond price."

More and more, Sigurd observed, we realize that *quiet* is important to our happiness. In our cities, the constant beat of strange and foreign wavelengths on our primal senses drives us to neuroticism. The din changes us from creatures who once knew the silences to fretful, uncertain beings "immersed in a cacophony of noise" that destroys sanity and equilibrium.

In recognition of this need for *quiet*, Sigurd Olson said, city churches leave their doors open so that people may come in off the streets and in the semidarkness find the *quiet* they need.

"I know a great sanctuary," Sigurd confided in his book *The Singing Wilderness*, "whose doors open onto one of the busiest and noisiest streets of the world. I go there whenever I pass, and as the doors close behind me and I look up to the stained glass windows, the quiet returns and I sense the silence once more. Beneath that vaulted dome is a small part of the eternal quiet the outside world once knew."

Beach the canoe, walk up the reedy shore, the pailful of fish heavy as concrete. The little greenie frogs go arching into the water, graceful as birds. Ah, how Mark Twain would have celebrated these jumping frogs. *Plop! Plop! Plooop!*

These plops and ploops are probably alerting every large-mouth bass this side of Arbor Vitae and as Steady notes, any bass that's been around longer than last Thursday has to associate the plopping and the plooping with incoming frogs as opposed to incoming coconuts. Are the bass out there now, lying in the weeds? *Plop! Plop! Plooop!* The frogs sound like Hula Poppers!

I feel a twinge of guilt about the greenie frogs. If I wasn't walking here, the frogs wouldn't be leaving here. It's like I forced them to walk the plank over waiting sharks.

Plop! Plop! Plooooop! And the frogs are all gone. Except one. I walk right up to it. It never moves. I bend, grab it and for the first time today I realize not everything is still as it once was. I see why the frog didn't move. I was approaching on its left side and the frog has no eye on its left side. No eye! No socket. Only skin. It couldn't see me.

Then, I walk very, *very* slowly along the reedy beach. There are more frogs like the eyeless one. Others have one leg deformed or missing altogether, the skin tight, unbroken. Many, many frogs with many anomalies.

Later I asked my professor friend at the university what causes that? Poison? Pesticides? He said it could be a lot of things and to bring him some of the greenie frogs next time. Then he read me what he called *his* "frog research."

One night, fishing from the pier
I felt a living presence near.
Turning to see, turning to hear
I saw the bullfrog on the beach.

His marsh lay on the farther shore
away from here by a mile or more.
But, this night he sat at our very door
silent, watching me. Just out of reach.

Above us, somebody's satellite flew by.
I do not know if it caught his eye.
I do not know if he watched the sky
and knew the stars, with a name for each.

Mute, we stayed as the night grew cold.
I felt then, Something. Something quite old.
Something familiar. Yet, Something untold.
Had he come to study? Had he come to teach?

After Steady Eddy read it, he said: "Well, when they don't *ribbit*, you gotta be a damned mind reader."

North Country Folks

Walt Goldsworthy, one of the North Country's most distinguished old-timers and a historian who could be sued on a regular basis if he published everything he knows about the folks in Vilas and Oneida counties, writes from his home territory in Three Lakes.

"Dear George:

"I have just finished reading your book *North Country Notebook*, which was given to me by your mother's good neighbor George Koller. Brother George I call him.

"It appears you and I have traveled the same path and touched bases and broken bread with the same personalities: Frank Lloyd Wright, Charlie and Nina Leopold Bradley and all the rest you mention. The only personality I don't know—and I don't recall reading any of his books—is Calvin Rutstrum. But Gordon MacQuarrie and even Harold (Bud) Jordahl I briefly touched.

"And of course, Father Himmelsbach. He was a very dear friend. One of the first I met when I came up here in 1946 was Father Himmelsbach. The other person was Windy Olson, the game warden.

"Priests and game wardens had little honor here in those days, but Windy and Father Joe left their marks during the years that followed and the country was the better for their passing this way. They were both very dear friends, along with Carl Marty of the Northernaire and a few others.

"I even had a 'Seven-Foot Nun' too. Our name for her was 'Old High-Power.' I remember her as a mean, frustrated, raw-boned creature who seemed to delight in wielding a 'tug,' or harness trace, especially to the boys. She kept getting more vicious with her leather-wielding until they shipped her out.

"I guess I am sort of a heretic. I'm a much better Christian than I am a Catholic! Like yourself, life's experiences and enlightening have been rewarding and I never was one given to blind loyalty to a political party, to a church or to a fraternity.

"The only exception I make is my loyalty to the Bible, which is a firm base that I hold to regardless of pope or preacher or devil. The religiosity of organized religion has turned me off.

"Now past the 'three score and ten,' I have witnessed all the credentials flaunted by man in his churches and in his politics, and all are finally exposed for what they are—weavings of the human mind.

"Incidentally, it was Windy Olson who first introduced me to your dad and mother. One year I was looking for a cabin

24

up here for Bob Becker, the outdoors columnist for the *Chicago Tribune*, and Windy suggested your folks' resort.

"I recall how concerned your mother was that Bob Becker 'could be rowdy' and she didn't want her cottage messed up. She was happy when she met Bob because he was a very quiet fellow.

"Also, your mother was interested in getting Walt Disney's Bambi as a logo for Three Lakes. I remember writing some letters for her about that.

"Listen. I was instrumental in getting the local Three Lakes Museum started years ago. Now, it's my hobby to keep me out of mischief. I mention this only because I think your book should do well at our museum shop.

"Keep fishing and writing! Thanks for the memories."

I believe Walt Goldsworthy implicitly when he says that my mother was concerned that Bob Becker "could be rowdy." My mother was always concerned that a resort guest "could be rowdy." I think it started the first year they had the resort and they rented a cabin for the whole summer to Shirley.

Shirley was from Antigo. She said her husband was in the army and sent her allotment checks and she just wanted to get away from the city heat for the summer. She was so delighted with this cool spot on Big Stone Lake—just 50 miles north of Antigo—that she insisted on paying three months' rent in advance. Well, it was just too good for the folks to pass up.

"Of course," Steady Eddy says, "knowing what we now know about those good-time people of Antigo, we would be chary and wary, but in those innocent, halcyon days, who knew?"

Shirley had a lot of visitors. Mostly they were male visitors, nicely dressed in suits and driving expensive, late-model cars. Shirley always said they were friends from the city.

Her friends never fished or swam or hiked through the woods. They always waved at the folks as they drove away, smiling. You never saw them again and you just figured Shirley had a lot of friends in the city.

Her cabin was the only one rented for the month of June and yet sometimes there were so many cars there, you'd swear the whole resort was full—and the city of Antigo was empty.

In town, the talk at the American Legion Bar was that prostitutes were working out of some area resorts and did we have one, too?

We never really found out for certain.

One unforgettable night in late June, a trucker in an 18-wheeler came to see Shirley and his truck got stuck in the filled-in marsh road. My mother said Shirley had to go and gave Shirley her money back.

Shirley wouldn't take the money. She said the rent was "too low anyway for such a high-class place." She drove off, smiling and waving. It took a day to get the truck out.

The rest of the summer was pretty quiet.

Go, and Sin No More!

Steady Eddy says you hear a lot of stories about folks being "born again" these days and it happened to his friend Tony.

"Tony," Steady said, "knew every piece of trout water in the whole state of Wisconsin and had fished most all of it. Tony said he even used to sneak into the army camp in the old days when they kept all the civilians out. He said he used to fish the trout creeks even while the National Guard units had their little maneuvers going on. He said he wore his camo fatigues in case anybody ever stopped him, but no one ever did and the trout fishing was great."

Tony might still be fishing there, Steady said, but with more and more guard units using the camp, it got noisier and noisier, especially when they started using helicopters on the field problems.

"Tony thought that the choppers put down the trout," Steady says. "He took to wearing earmuffs in the summer. This was in the Olden Days before Walkman, where you could wear a headset everywhere and just tune the whole world out. If Tony had a Walkman he might still be fishing those army trout, but of course, if he had he wouldn't have found God the way he did. Because just about the time the noise level was up to his eyebrows, Tony heard about another place where the trouting might not be too shabby and a friend told him *this* place was so quiet you thought you were in church. 'An *empty* church.'

"As a matter of fact, this place turned out to be an old Catholic seminary that had fallen on hard times because not so many young Catholic men were going into the priesthood these days and the church was renting out the buildings for conferences and meetings and even looking for buyers, no matter, Tony pointed out, 'their religious persuasion.'

"Of course," Steady noted, "if the church had let women become priests as some women were suggesting, maybe the seminary would be full up again. But that's probably an idea that's still a little bit revolutionary.

"Anyway, the church was having a hard time selling off the property because all the prospective buyers said the price was just too high, considering all the work they said the place needed. It wasn't a hotel. It wasn't apartments.

"What it was, Tony said, was your basic old-timey seminary. Kind of like army barracks with partitions. The rooms were all itty-bitty cells meant for study and meditation and sleeping, and the talk was that you'd have to knock out walls and enlarge the quarters, replaster, rewire, repaint, put in new plumbing, bathrooms, showers, just the basic stuff for habitation."

You got the idea it was pretty rundown and needed a lot of rehabbing.

"Anyway," Steady said, "Tony heard there were only a couple of people living there now. A caretaker couple who look after the place and keep an eye out for vandals. And then, there was this old priest who has chosen to live out his retirement in one of the little cottages down in the glen."

Steady recalled that at that point Tony got that look he always got when the evening trout started puddling the surface like a bubbling pudding.

"Guess why the little old priest lives in that little old cottage all alone," Tony had asked, "instead of in a home with all the other old priests?"

"Because he snores?" Steady had said.

"Because," Tony said, "that little cottage is on a pond, and the pond is full of trout, and the old priest is *an old trout fisherman!*"

"What kind of trout?"

"Rainbow trout. The friend who told me said these are not your pasty-fleshed hatchery fish raised on pellets and dumb as doughnuts. These are honest-to-God authentic RAINBOW TROUT, wilder than hares and deep-bellied as carp."

Tony told Steady that when his friend first saw the trout, he thought: "My God! This is what the Catholic church means when it talks about 'Holy Water.' "

Tony and his friend always intended to sneak into the old priest's pond—"the Church of the Holy Rainbow" they called it—but the friend got transferred by his company to Houston. Tony found the old priest's trout pond by himself and the first time he sneaked in, the old priest found him: An old beagle sniffing out a young rabbit.

"This was a law-and-order priest," Steady said. "He just railed about private property and trespass and if he ever saw Tony there again, he would forget about being charitable and just press charges against him, dammit!

"That's when Tony told the priest he was a fallen-away Catholic, which he was. He begged the priest to hear his confession. He begged to be permitted to return to Holy Mother Church. Could this kind, godly man make it possible?

" 'Spoken,' the priest said, 'like a true trout fisherman, which is to say like the born liars that we are! I KNOW why you're doing this.' Tony said yes, he would sneak into the pond every chance he got, but he would NOT KEEP ANY TROUT. EVER! They started like that and eventually Tony didn't have to sneak and they fished together for years until the old priest died. He left Tony his bamboo rod and every Sunday morning they still fish the pond together. Tony says, as the old trout fishermen knew, it is like going to church."

A New Way to Spell Relief

They were sitting around at the American Legion Bar up in Three Lakes the other night—"just trying to put a little zip into things" is the way Steady Eddy puts it—and they got to discussing the newest development in the high-tech world of trout fishing: chest-high waders that come with a zippered fly front.

"Well, you know," Gene the bartender was saying, "this invention is gonna get a lot of laughs and sniggers from a lot of people who don't know any better, namely, people who have never been up to their wazoo in cold, clammy waders when the Call of Nature comes and you have to struggle out of the current, struggle up the stream bank and lower your waders to half-mast in order not to spoil your morning, not to mention your L.L. Bean chinos.

"Then, having done your business, you reverse the procedure, get back into the pool and, dry as vermouth, resume your fishing. Only now, you've spooked every trout that was in the pool when you started for shore, like a plunging water buffalo, stirring up in the process enough sediments to send thousands of nymphs downstream and trigger a feeding frenzy that makes a hex hatch seem as tame as the good Father Himmelsbach's cribbage game.

"I was reading a story in the paper by Robert McNeil of the United Press, and you could tell right away that old Bob has been up to his hips with our common problem. He was writing about a company that invented a waterproof fly for chest waders. 'The guy who invented a waterproof fly for chest waders,' old Bob says, 'will be an INSTANT millionaire.' Well, I say that guy deserves it. This could be the greatest invention since the church key, and I don't mean the one that unlocks the front door of St. Theresa's."

Gene waited for reaction from his customers, all two of them: the good priest and the good doctor.

"If this be true," Doc said, "it is greater than the church key. It is *greater* than the astronauts' solution, which must really be to pee in your pants in some high-tech fashion. It is greater than Porta-Potty. Getting caught with your pants up can be a bigger trauma than getting caught with them down. And coming out of a trout stream with your waders full is far worse than coming out with your creel empty. Who has brought this miracle to pass—if I might coin a phrase?"

"The Simms company of Jackson Hole, Wyoming," Gene said, "which has been making top-grade stocking-foot neoprene waders for several years now, aimed at the flyfishing market. A little play on words there."

"Especially if you're a seventh grade boy," Doc said.

"Tending bar at the Legion," Father Himmelsbach added.

"This Simms zipper," Gene continued, "is not confined to the crotch area. It extends all the way to the top of the waders, which means that they can be opened for ventilation and easy on, easy off. This zipper, you know, is a modification of the special waterproof one made for scuba divers' dry suits."

"I never thought about divers coming out of the water to pee," Doc said.

"We got a man here," Gene said, "licensed by a sovereign state to operate on people, and we now discover that he has about as much imagination as a bag of Beer Nuts."

"I assume," Doc said, "that this trendy little item has been priced for the yuppies who just LOVE trout fishing because the gear can cost more than all the fixtures in the Legion and you get to wear it ALL every time you sally forth to the creeks in your dusty BMW."

"Well," Gene said, "the Simms product manager, Mr. Bill Klyn, says that his firm can supply the zipper enclosure for $75 extra on all Simms neoprene stocking-foot waders. The retail cost of the waders is about $225, so you're looking at about $300 for a pair of waders."

"I'm not looking at them," Doc sniffed. "Seventy-five dollars for a zipper is ridiculous."

"That's right," Father Himmelsbach said. "Ridiculous. It's like $100 for a tonsil."

"What's to stop me," Doc asked, "from taking my old patched-up canvas waders into our friendly shoemaker and asking her to please sew in a waterproof zipper?"

"Ah," Gene said, "you have really asked *two* questions there, Doc. The answer to the first is that only a good malpractice suit will ever stop you, and don't think that the more aggrieved members of this community aren't seriously considering going that route.

"The answer to your second question is that your friendly shoemaker, who, it must be admitted, stitches better than most surgeons that I know, can't really sew in this zipper. Bill Klyn says that 'bonding' is the biggest problem with the zipper. Simms has discovered a way of bonding with a 'certain adhesive.' Now, if you think you can get by with Krazy Glue, that's up to you.

"Klyn also says that most major wader manufacturers making canvas or PVC waders are simply not going to look at a high-end, expensive wader like this one."

"So," Doc said, "either you deal with Mr. Klyn's folks for your waders with the zipper or you go through life with a wet foot, so to speak."

"Well," Gene said slyly, "you could have used *buttons* on a wader fly, only you lost all yours."

"A toast," Doc said. "To the fly-front wader. Can the trapdoor wader be far behind?"

Father Himmelsbach said Amen to that. Gene shook a leg.

The Widow's Return

When I first began hanging out with the Garage Sale Junkie, we never stopped at a place where the sign said ANTIQUES FOR SALE. Steady Eddy says it was because on the circuits we traveled nobody could spell "Antiques," and we were always stopping at places where the signs said RUMMAGE or GARAGE SALE or YARD SALE or ESTATE SALE or sometimes just JUNQUE!

"Antiques" was a buzzword, the Junkie said. It meant that you were going to pay a pretty penny because you were dealing with sophisticated folks who had been around the block once or twice.

"There are no rubes left anymore," Bob Hope observed once. "TV has turned everybody into city slickers."

The love of the Junkie's life was your basic second-hand stuff—"twice-loved toys" as the sentimental among us are fond of saying, but the sentimental among us does not include the Garage Sale Junkie.

She wasn't on some nostalgia trip out there. She was shopping for bargains, true, but the bargains had to be stuff we could USE in our daily lives.

The stuff has included teapots, wine glasses, a fur coat from Russia—or was it Romania?—boxes of books, boxes of Legos, and even a couple of Coleman lanterns to show me what treasures were waiting out there for the curiosity-seeker will-

31

ing to just GO and start sniffing around like a beagle pup put out to piddle. So, I began sniffing a little.

It was the long Wisconsin winters that got the Junkie to finally stop at places that said ANTIQUES. She was suffering the agonies of the damned. I think Cub fans are like that in the winter. Of course, Cub fans are like that in the summer, too. The Junkie was climbing the walls on the weekends until she finally gave in and off we went to the places with the AN-TIQUES signs, places that are called ANTIQUES MALLS.

One of her favorites on the "route" now is over in Co-lumbus. It used to be a big cannery and it employed most of the town folks who had "put up" peas and beans and corn ever since Adam was a pup. When the cannery closed, a local boy who worked there, Norm Hageman, decided to take it over rather than see it, and the town, die.

The building is 12,000 square feet, and Norm and his wife, Virginia, decided to put in an ANTIQUES MALL. They rent space to around 50 different sellers, and they offer not only "antiques" but "collectibles" as well. Everything from baseball cards—I don't think the Billy Ripkin card is there, yet—to Betty Boop dolls and all that stuff that Steady Eddy says "YOU grew up with—and like a dummy THREW AWAY!"

The last time we drove over, there was melt and there was drizzle and there was Norm shoveling the water out of a low spot in the parking lot. The Good Old Boys up at the American Legion Bar in Three Lakes just love that, their theory being that anybody who knows how to shovel water doesn't have to prove anything by walking on it.

Inside, the Garage Sale Junkie was sniffing out the candle snuffers and holders. I got myself hooked in the section marked FISHING LURES.

There were *a lot of wooden* fishing lures—"plugs," the Old Man used to call them—and most of them were painted red and white. White bodies, red heads because the experts in those days swore that red and white was the deadliest com-bination for everything in Wisconsin waters: muskie, bass, northern pike. Even walleye on red-and-white Junebug spin-ners. Of course, perch scale finish was good too. That's what the early Pikie Minnows and River Runts were.

I stared and stared at those old-timey plugs—and Bango! I was back at Little Saint Germain Lake watching the Old Man casting from the pier at Sisson's Resort on Highway 70. Then this tourist came down and started casting, too. He was standing way too close and he was casting sidearm and sure enough, he hooked the Old Man in the back of the head with a Bass-Oreno. It was red and white. I remember screaming.

The tourist almost fainted—and so did I—because the treble hooks were in so deep you couldn't see the barbs. The Old Man told him to cut the line and told me to get my mother to drive to the doctor. All the while the Old Man was holding a towel to his head because he was bleeding badly. The blood soaked through the towel. When he came back, he gave the Bass-Oreno to the tourist and said they were still friends, but the man should learn to cast *overhead*.

Then I was back in Columbus, about to buy the Bass-Oreno, when I saw the Weedless Widow! Red head, white body, bucktail covering the single rear hook, which was protected by a wire weed-guard.

THE WEEDLESS WIDOW! The plug of plugs!

All that sun-filled pre-army summer, I had flung a Weedless Widow over every weedbed in the Chain of Lakes. It took black bass, northerns, muskies. It was the best damn surface bait in the weeds I ever found and that included the best in tough lily pads, too. You couldn't hang it up! I never lost one out on the water. I lost them here on the land somewhere, with my baseball cards and my boyhood.

Turning that wondrous lure in my hand, I was back in that wooden round-bottom in the sloughs of Planting Ground Lake, squinting against the sun, wearing just a swimsuit and sunglasses, watching, whooping as the huge fish smashed that Weedless Widow on the surface and sailed into the sky with it. I knew then that I was going to live forever.

The Weedless Widow was priced at $12.50. Oh TOO HIGH, I thought. The Junkie made me buy it. "Listen," she said, "you'll use it in your daily life."

SUMMER

Skinny-Dip

The lake is so tiny you can't find it on most maps. No road leads to it; you have to walk in from a fire lane in the forest. There isn't a cottage, a cabin, a shack, or a beer can on the whole shore.

The only sign of humans for miles around is the water-filled flatbottom boat, half-sunken and hidden away in the shallows under the sheltering branches of balsam.

The boat is wooden, a working relic of another era, as are the two grown-up little boys who have been hiding it here for years. One is the good priest and the other is the good doctor.

Indoors they usually are to be found at the American Legion bar in the North Country town not too far from here.

The bar is renowned for its bartender named Gene, who sleeps in his Chicago Cubs cap; for its ancient cribbage board, worn and polished as the Old Man's hickory ax handle; and for its beer cooler where, once a week, the Good Old Boys get into their snowmobile suits and Sorel boots, sit themselves down on the full kegs and just stay that way, practicing for ice fishing.

The tiny little lake has no official name. Some of the old-timers used to call it Spring Lake. Others called it Gin Lake because it was so clear. None of those old-timers are around anymore. The good doctor and the good priest are about the only humans who even come to the lake these days, let alone know how to find it.

The doctor, dependent upon his mood, has been known to refer to the tiny lake as either "The Bass Hole" or "The Little Chapel of the Big Bass."

"Well, Father," Doc will say in mixed company, "as the Seven-Foot Nun always used to say: 'A little time in the chapel will do wonders for your soul.' "

Father Himmelsbach always takes that as an inside joke, especially if it is said in the presence of Illinois people who have bought lake property on the Chain of Lakes and have landscaped with plastic pink flamingos and cast-iron white-tailed deer.

The doctor and the priest have been visiting the little lake together since they were boys before "WW Two," as Gene puts it. Doc was not a *real* doctor then—Gene says that there is a question if he's a *real* doctor now—and Father Himmelsbach was an altar boy when all the responses were in Latin and nobody had ever heard of a "guitar mass."

Doc's grandpa had taken the two of them to the bass lake on the condition that they "cross their hearts and swear to die" if they ever told another living soul.

They never did—not even after Doc's grandpa died and they inherited, by default, the wooden flatbottom, a set of wooden oars and a cement-filled paint can that Grandpa used for an anchor.

When they were little, Doc and Father Himmelsbach learned to fish these bass with Grandpa's cane poles, and they have preserved those poles with love and varnish as though they were the relics of a saint.

"Which," Father Himmelsbach, who knows about such things, says, "indeed they are."

The cane poles are still rigged and ready to go and can be hauled out of their semiretirement in Doc's garage on a moment's notice as indeed they have been when nostalgia has gotten the better of them. Then they tie the bundle of poles on top of Doc's old Chrysler fish-car with a red bandanna on the southern end to warn any traffic following of their oversize load.

"God," Doc always says when they do that, "I feel like we're hauling logs to the mill."

Now they sat in the drifting flatbottom, working the lily pads with their fly rods and poppers. Doc was raised on the fly rod because his father loved to fish trout, and Doc taught Father Himmelsbach how to use a fly rod on bass "instead of a derrick."

"Who else," Gene says at the Legion bar, "could convert a priest?"

The bass smashed the little poppers and fought furiously in "the lettuce fields," as Doc called the slough. More than one fish wrapped itself around the ropelike lily-pad stems and broke itself off. Doc said he wanted only enough fillets to drop off for the Widow Elvira on the way home.

The priest smiled. In all seasons, he has helped Doc fill the Widow Elvira's freezer with enough fish fillets, partridge, and venison steaks to see her through another marriage, if she was so inclined. "And, of course," Father Himmelsbach has advised Doc on more than one provisioning trip, "she is so inclined."

"Inclined or reclined," Doc growls, "I am not about to marry again, and neither is she. We're just a couple of friends from the old days. God, on a date once, when I just came back from the army, we started out for a movie and then just sat and talked and wound up skinny-dipping."

"No wonder she married someone else," the priest said.

"You know, Joe," Doc said, "that's the funny part about growing old. Inside this ancient shell is that 21-year-old kid just rattling around in there like a beagle pup and, yet, here I am—*here we are*—like a couple of old geezers, hats down around our ears, shoes laced up tight. Hell! When was the last time either of us went skinny-dipping?"

They fished in silence for a long time. When they had enough, Father Himmelsbach rowed them into shore and, without a word, took off his shoes and his clothes and waded out into the lake. He dived, came up sputtering, then swam around while Doc started to fillet the bass. Doc always fillets the fish because, as he says, "Nobody else here went to med school."

The priest was huffing and puffing and sputtering out there and Doc kept up a running commentary as he cleaned the fish.

"Remember, Joe," he yelled, "hockey was your sport. You liked the water hard so you couldn't fall through it." And: "If you drown, can I do the last rites?" and "If you did this on Sunday, you could collect a lot of money. This is better than Bingo!"

When Doc finished with the fillets, he had to pull up the boat and load the car by himself because Father Himmelsbach still was trying to dry off in the late afternoon sun, now dipping below the pines. The priest was shivering, but he wasn't wheezing too badly.

"I should have brought a towel," he said.

"All you guys think God will provide," Doc said, "so you go off the deep end. Next time, we'll bring a couple."

"Well," the priest said, "when was the last time *you* went skinny-dipping?"

"I think," Doc said, "I better sharpen up the fillet knives. If you don't get that hernia taken care of, you're going to need a creel to carry it around in."

When they stopped by at the Widow Elvira's, she just went on and on about the bass fillets and how "professional" they always looked. She put them in the freezer next to the venison steaks, which were equally "professional" looking. Then she took out two cans of lemonade because she knew that Gene wouldn't be caught dead serving lemonade at his precious American Legion Bar—even if someone asked for it, which wasn't likely.

When they settled in around her kitchen table, she noticed that Father Himmelsbach's hair was wet.

"My," she said, "it looks as though he fell in."

"It does look that way," Doc said, "doesn't it?"

"I didn't fall," Father Himmelsbach said. "I was pushed."

Doc raised his lemonade and they drank to that.

Trout Bum

How would you describe a grown man who drove his car to the banks of a Wisconsin trout stream one April a few years ago, then just lived there in the car all summer long, tying flies in the front seat, sleeping in the back seat and fishing trout like an otter?

"I guess," Tom Wendelburg says at the fly-tying vise in the house where he now lives in Middleton, "if you described me as a 'trout fishing bum,' that would be accurate."

Most of Wendelburg's acquaintances, for whom he has tied his amazingly productive trout flies, do not quarrel with that description.

Others have had a nose full of Wendelburg's smothering ability to submerge them in the torrent of his trout exploits and hold them like a fish on a tight line, drowning in silent anger and frustration. Sometimes, not so silent. They tell you in no uncertain terms what they think of Tom Wendelburg.

Steve Born is one of Wendelburg's trout-fishing buddies and a longtime Wendelburg watcher. It's the next best thing, Born insists, to watching for the annual mayfly eruption—the fabulous "hexagenia hatch"—on "Sand County" rivers like the Mecan. When he isn't hanging out with Wendelburg, Born is a professor and heads the water resources management program at the University of Wisconsin-Madison. He also is past president of Trout Unlimited's southern chapter.

"Wendelburg," Born says, "can drive people right up the wall. He can talk your arm off. Not to mention your leg and waders. A lot of pretty good trout fishermen think they know as much about trout fishing as Wendelburg does, but Wendelburg doesn't think so."

"I consider myself an expert," Wendelburg says straight out. "I don't think I can be outfished by too many people in the world with a fly rod."

He probably can't be outwritten by too many people in the world, either, when it comes to a technical story on trout fishing. He has published more than 100 articles in such national magazines as *Field & Stream, Outdoor Life, Fly Fisherman, Trout* and a creel full of others. He may be infamous, but he's also famous.

"When he writes about trout fishing," Born says, "it's like the trout are talking to you."

Wendelburg doesn't write as much as he used to. He developed a writer's block as big as a beaver house in 1982. It wasn't exactly "burnout," but suddenly he had no words and no money and that's when he decided to live in his car on that trout stream west of Madison. He supported himself—"more or less," some observers would say—by selling hand-tied flies to passing fisher folk.

"I got a piece of driftwood," he remembers, "and put a fly-tying vise on it. I snugged it up under the steering wheel with my knees and tied flies right in the car. I made a pretty good going of selling trout flies out of my car because my flies are so good."

"He's right, of course," Steve Born says. "But, with some people, that goes over like a chain saw in church. They *know* his flies are good. They just don't want him *saying* that his flies are so good."

But the market for trout flies can rise and fall like a trout stream. At low water, Wendelburg is not above hooking a friend for an occasional loan. Tom, some friends agree, can be forgetful about loans. Some friends have been known to cringe when Tom appears on a trout stream. They reel in quickly and slink away into the brush, even if good fish have been rising.

Some friends say they sometimes feel Wendelburg regards all his flies as HIS flies. "There's the Wendelburg leech and the Wendelburg scud and it's just inconceivable to Tom that any of these flies could have originated with anybody else. That's the Wendelburg paranoia."

His writing has brought him fame but not fortune. "The writing income has never been much," Wendelburg concedes. "In fact, it was embarrassingly small, and if I were to tell you about what the big famous fishing writers make—writers I know personally—it would be embarrassing to them because what they make is embarrassingly small."

Wendelburg admits that his trout fishing is an all-consuming passion, an addiction, and that he doesn't know how he got this way. As a youngster growing up in Milwaukee—he was born there in 1943—he lived across the street from the Washington Park lagoon.

"I was over there all the time," he recalls, "and I just developed a tremendous fascination for fish and water."

On the way home from school, instead of going to church choir practice, he would detour over to the park and watch the sunfish and the rock bass for hours, he says. He caught his

first fish there when he was five—a three-and-a-half-inch bluegill on a cane pole. "With a string and a worm on a bent pin,"
he smiles, "just like out of some storybook."

By the time he was ten, he was casting flat-fish lures with
a spinning rod and catching largemouth bass in the three-pound
range. Then he discovered a way of fishing that truly hooked
him for life.

"I came upon this fly rod," he says with reverence. "It
was a nine-foot telescoping tubular steel thing that weighed
about three pounds. I put an all-silk crack-fly line on it. I had
done a lot of reading and all the trout writers said that was
what you needed."

Young Wendelburg got himself an old fly-tying kit and
the very first flies he fished with were of his own making. They
fooled a lot of unsophisticated bluegills and sunfish.

"I learned then," he admits, "that seven-inch to nine-inch
black bass were much craftier and took a lot more work to
catch."

You had to tie brown over yellow streamer flies to get the
bass even to give you a look. Wendelburg tied them that way
and decided that they probably looked like little darting minnows to the bass because they put the bass into a feeding frenzy.
The streamer ties changed his daylight fishing.

"Then I stayed late and fished," he recalls, "and lo and
behold, I would get splashy strikes after dark. That's how I
invented crappie fishing after dark. I was nine or ten at the
time."

Steve Born smiles and shakes his head.

"It's like Jelly Roll Morton saying he invented jazz," Born
says. "But who's to say they didn't?"

Wendelburg graduated from Brookfield Central High
School, went on to get a journalism degree at the University
of Wisconsin-Madison in 1965 and was hired by the *Idaho State
Journal* in Pocatello as a police and general assignment reporter. He had "surveyed" all the newspapers in the Rocky
Mountain area that were near good trout fishing, since one of
his ambitions was to fish the western rivers and catch the bigger
trout. The other ambition was to rub elbows with all the big-
name trout writers he had been reading since he was a kid.

41

He was doing both when Brookfield Central asked him to return as a teacher of journalism and English. He says proudly that he accepted and stayed four years, through 1969.

"I got married earlier," Wendelburg goes on to say, "I think it was 1965 or '66—I forget exactly—and our honeymoon tent took us to places like the Bighorn Mountains in Wyoming and to Henry's Fork of the Snake River in Idaho."

In 1967 Wendelburg started taking graduate courses in summer school at the University of Montana in Missoula and the newlyweds set up housekeeping in a 17-foot trailer by Rock Creek, "a blue-ribbon trout stream."

Wendelburg claims that the University of Montana then told him that he could not complete his master's degree in summer school programs "as they said I could when they got me to go out there." He nibbled at a few classes but he had lost his appetite for formal journalism education.

Rock Creek and the Montana trout waters became his graduate school. He studied insect hatches, tied flies, caught the big western trout. The trout so impressed his ranch owner/ landlord that he persuaded Wendelburg to guide him and, at that moment, Wendelburg "turned pro," as he put it.

He opened a little fly shop and developed an Orvis fishing-equipment dealership. He admits that he got a lot of very expensive equipment cut-rate.

(His favorite rod today is an Orvis 2-Weight that he fishes with a 3-Double tapered line on a Hardy Flea-Weight reel. He has taken a 27-inch brown trout with the 2-Weight.)

In Montana, Wendelburg guided clients from all over the country and was teaching them, ever so subtly, of course, to fish his way, preferably with his hand-tied flies that could be purchased at his fly shop or on the stream when the clients couldn't catch diddly. Wendelburg took pride in teaching them.

"I even taught my wife to flyfish," he says.

She had been a drama teacher when they met. She entered his world further when she did the photography for his fishing articles. "She became a very, very accomplished fisher-woman," he says, beaming. "Excellent, in fact."

But, as anyone who has ever tried it knows, Wendelburg's world isn't for everyone.

The marriage lasted only slightly longer than a salmon-fly hatch. They divorced in Missoula, and Wendelburg returned to the UW. He enrolled in graduate school but the old appetite for academics was gone and he dropped out to write his trout pieces.

"I moved out to Cross Plains," he says, "and went into writing full time." He also went into trout fishing full time. Working part time, he already had sold 50 articles.

The first article he sold as a full timer was on flyfishing Black Earth Creek. *Outdoor Life* magazine bought it and Wendelburg was launched as "the most prolific technical writer on trout to come out of Wisconsin." He fished trout; he wrote trout stories; he tied trout flies. He was living the life he had dreamed about back on the banks of the lagoon at Washington Park. He also was studying his beloved trout the way some scholars study their beloved Shakespeare.

"I walk the trout streams constantly," he says, "in all months of the year, looking for trout, enjoying my time, learning something, whatever I can.

"I don't carry a rod, but I carry flies in my wallet, my own flies I designed: my scud flies, my sow bugs, a few streamers. I also carry a spool of sewing thread and I pick up willow sticks and fish these contraptions in the culverts and along the edges. God, I've caught some beautiful trout doing this. I release them, of course. Now I kill almost no trout."

He has written a few new trout pieces lately, but he still struggles with that pesky writer's block.

"Sometimes," he says, "I think the real problem is that I've written everything I have to say. That's it. It's over. I've said it all."

Perhaps. His friend Born feels that even if Wendelburg never writes another fishing word, his published articles—if only some book publisher thought to collect them—could become a trout-fishing classic.

"Wendelburg on Trout," Born muses. "He's a hell of a teacher. Last year WHA-TV's 'Wisconsin Magazine' program followed him right into a stream catching fish. They called the segment 'Hooked on Trout.' Wendelburg showing you how he does it. Talking right to you. It's one of the greatest trout videos you'll ever see."

Wendelburg coughs his smoker's hack—he is not only hooked on trout, he is hooked on cigarets, too—and goes back to his fly-tying vise in the damp basement at his Middleton home. His life's work is stacked in metal filing cabinets and cardboard boxes cluttered in the damp along one wall.

It's all here. Everything you always wanted to know about trout. About fishing. About dedication. About fixation. About true love.

He is finishing an order of twenty dozen nymphs, an all-marabou creation for Doug Swisher's annual national catalog.

He coughs, squints in the smoke. The stub of a cigaret clinging to his lips could be one of his hand-tied grubs.

"This writer's-block thing," he says, "is something. I have to temper that with my attitude. I'm getting a bit older. I'm not making any money. I don't think I'll ever make any—unless somebody hires me for a retainer."

Many of Wendelburg's acquaintances have talked about saving him from the "trout bum's disease."

"But, based on my observations," Born says, "we haven't been able to save him because he has contaminated all of us. Some of Wendelburg's saviors have even discussed—out loud—the possibilities of joining him. There are people on this very faculty who would do that in a minute. But to do that takes something Wendelburg has—and we don't."

"Anybody can join me," Wendelburg insists. "All you have to do is call (608) 831-6969 in Middleton and hire me. I'll tie up some flies for you to buy, find some fish for you to catch and pretty much tell you what I know about trout."

If Wendelburg tells you only a little bit of what he knows about trout fishing, Born says, it will fill your creel with more than you want to carry.

When he tells you more about what he knows, you—like most of his other pupils—will leave your creel at home and keep the fish in your heart.

A Ship of Fools

It'a hard for those of us who get up and go to work to realize that there are other folks around—rich folks—who, once they get up, have to figure what they're going to do with their day, because they sure don't have to go to work.

The North Country has always attracted its share of the idle rich, from the olden times, when a Chris-Craft was the ultimate status symbol, surpassed only by the two-story boathouse in which you parked it.

The sons of the rich were always a particular bane to those of us who were sons of the poor.

"God," Gene Step used to lament at the American Legion Bar in Three Lakes, "they come up for the summer with the suntans they got down in Florida." Or Acapulco. Or Bimini. Or Honolulu.

The old rich, who made all the money in the first place, usually didn't throw their weight or their wealth around. A lot of them drove into town from their lakeshore estates—and this is not "estates" in the Chicago realtor sense of the word. This is one rich guy owning thousands of acres, a half-dozen private lakes and servants' quarters for the only black people this side of Milwaukee. Unless you count Green Bay, which for years prided itself on having one black family in town, before Vince Lombardi took over the hapless Packers and started building the defensive unit that did for Green Bay what the hedgehog formations did for the Roman Empire, namely, crack open the heads and backs of all who took up arms against it.

The old rich came into town in pickup trucks and chino shirts and pants looking for all the world like retired game wardens or forest rangers. It was their sons who never let you forget who could buy and sell the American Legion Bar in a minute, and with all of us in it to boot.

One time, on the gravel bar in Big Stone, the Old Man and I were fishing walleyes after sunset, and all of a sudden the biggest boat I had seen in my life just loomed up over us, its running lights stuck high up in the night sky like the warning lights on radio towers.

This is the way it ends, I thought. We're going to be rammed within sight of home by an aircraft carrier that has somehow wound up not only in the middle of the Old Man's lake but, indeed, in the middle of the Old Man's lap.

An electric motor hummed in the darkness, a great cannonball splash washed over our gunwales and a blinding searchlight flooded us in cold light. (You bet, Steady Eddy would say later. It's the classic attack. First the depth charges, then the deck guns. It's the way the rich work.)

Then a figure appeared at the starboard rail, and a voice—half-God, half-nasal—boomed through the bullhorn: "Ahoy, down there. How they bitin'?"

The Old Man mumbled something in a foreign language.

I was too stunned to answer. And besides, as Steady Eddy pointed out later, they were too far away to hear me anyway.

Another kid joined the bullhorn at the railing, and then two minnows came down on two lines and plunked into the water inches from us.

"Geez," the Old Man said. "They're fishing closer to our boat than we are."

They kept up a running chatter with us. They were the floor show and we were the floor. It was outrageous and they knew it.

There were these two locals fishing, their retelling would begin, *and you talk about somebody being scared shitless. . . .* There were all kinds of variations, and they all wound up, sooner or later, at the American Legion, at the Chalet, and at the Showboat.

I don't think the Old Man and I caught another fish that night, and there were walleyes going up to the Queen Mary like they were in elevators. You'd crane your neck and watch fish disappear into the sky like birds.

The Old Man couldn't get over it. It was the biggest god-damn boat that was ever seen on the Chain of Lakes. Somebody said the kids had it trucked over from Lake Superior just for the hell of it while their old man was away, because fishing out of the little Chris-Craft runabout was duller than hell, and the locals could look down on them for that. Well, nobody could look down on them in their aircraft carrier except God.

"Boy," the Old Man marveled, "it must be like fishing from the bridge at Winneconne."

The old rich sure knew where all the good hunting and fishing were, and they bought up all the land to make damn sure they controlled it.

Gene Step said it was a classic pattern.

"The British have been doing that for centuries," he said. "That's what really built the British Empire. It was the rich roaming the boonies, locking up all the world's great salmon rivers."

It didn't make the Norskis at the bar any happier to hear that, even in their beloved homeland today, some of the best fishing beats were in the hands of the Great Blue-Eyed Salmon Seekers.

"I think that's what distinguished the Brits from your ordinary run of Huns and Vandals," Gene said as we settled in our side of the bar. "The usual conquerors were out for the usual booty. But pillaging pales after a while, and then corruption gnaws on the empire like mildew in your old canvas creel. The Brits aspired to the higher values."

"Salmon," the Norskis chorused.

"Exactly so," Gene said. "Salmon."

Even the Seven-Foot Nun tracing the geopolitical expansion of Holy Mother Church had never drawn a more vivid picture of conquest.

"The Spaniards came for gold," Gene said. "The French came for beaver pelts. The Norskis came for the view. But the Brits . . ."

We looked around the American Legion, and there wasn't a Brit in the place. I don't think there has ever been one. There must be a moral in there somewhere. Or, as Steady says: *a morale.*

Goblins Lurk below the Surface

The canoe was at the edge of the lily pads and I was being very mindful of my casts, dropping the bug away from the jungle of fronds and stalks that were stronger than rope and tougher than wire.

There was no wind. The water was still. The lily bed was flat as a kitchen floor. When you're fishing bass with a bug— or any surface lure—this is a situation pregnant with possibilities.

The gurgling, slurping, plunking, *ploop, pop, ploop, pop* of the bug was looking and sounding very much like something in distress out there. Something not robust and healthy as a horse, but something injured, wounded—pausing much in its progress to rest and gather itself and then resume its limping, perilous journey, askew and disoriented, along the shadowy green abyss where the monsters dwell out of the sunlight.

You have to be very watchful and focused in this fishing, for the mind tends to stray and you find yourself daydreaming. While that may be restful, it does not prepare you for the sheer shock of a large bass exploding under your very nose like a grenade.

When you are not expecting a hand grenade, the explosion causes your heart to race like a runaway engine—your temples pound, your breath comes right out of your pores and your mouth fills with a fear you can taste.

The unknown can fill your mind with goblins. The unexpected can cause you to fill your pants.

Up at the American Legion Bar in Three Lakes, they talk of the muskie fishermen, fishing alone, found dead in their boats or in the water. The speculation is that the dead fisherman wasn't watchful and focused on his spluttering bait coming in, and a muskie exploded under his nose and stopped his heart and caused him to topple over, and now he is focused forever.

I remember the time I was rowing the Old Man along the weed beds of Big Stone while he cast a wooden Bass-Oreno for muskies. The tea-brown waters of the Chain of Lakes gave any red-and-white lure a spooky yellowish look, and I always shivered just thinking of all that spooky deep water under our feet.

When we anchored for walleyes off the gravel bar, the clothesline of the anchor rope evoked the same chilly feeling in me. The white rope curved away into the depths of dark tea and then disappeared, and my mind ran riot just thinking of what was down there in the dark, watching us.

Granted, this was in what Steady Eddy is pleased to call my "parochial school period," when my inner space was populated with more goblins than a bat cave and we stuck to the Seven-Foot Nun like glue because she could look any goblin straight in the eye and face it right down, including Father Kohler, who was just another seventh-grade boy as far as she was concerned.

One time when I was rowing the Old Man on Big Stone, a gust of wind came up and blew the flatbottom right out of my control toward the weed bed, and that's when I realized the wind was stronger than I was, and that was as fearful as the tea-brown waters beginning to roll.

Seeing my plight, the Old Man reeled in very quickly, watching the wind defeating me, and as he reached to grab an oar, the Bass-Oreno came flying over the gunwale in a hurried arc and right behind it, chasing it, a small muskie with its mouth open to strike. The mouth was an alligator mouth.

The fish hit the Old Man in the chest, and his mouth opened as wide as the muskie's. The muskie fell onto the floor-boards and was thrashing against the Old Man's tackle box with its greenish body.

I remember being very panicked because I thought that we were going to tip over for sure and we were all going into the tea-brown waters, which were now rolling and angry.

The Old Man reeled the Bass-Oreno right up to the swivel of the wire leader, put the rod down, let us drift into the weed bed and turned his attention to the muskie. He picked it up with both hands, held it alongside the wooden yardstick that was nailed to the gunwale, and very coolly measured it.

Muskies had to be 30 inches long in those days, and I would have sworn to God that this one was that big for sure. I would have sworn he was a foot bigger.

The Old Man was holding that living muskie like he was a taxidermist in Eagle River. The Old Man and the muskie both seemed to be smiling. I wish we had brought the folding Kodak camera along, but I never took the camera fishing.

The Old Man swung the muskie over the gunwale and lowered it into the water. The fish finned for only a second and then, with a flip of its tail, it shot down into the tea-brown depths and disappeared.

The Old Man washed off his hands in the water and was laughing.

"Too small," he said. "Not legal. Not smart, either."

He got us out of the weed bed, got me straightened around on the oars and went back to casting out the Bass-Oreno.

Because he wasn't afraid, I lost my fear, and then I was laughing too, but as I rowed I really got transfixed by the wet spot on his shirt, and I was just relieved that the fish had hit him in the chest and not me.

I wasn't focused in those days, but watching him I learned how important focus was. Well, I was focused now. Watching the bug, I asked the Old Man to send me a fish.

THE LEGION BAR

Snoredom

They were sitting around the American Legion Bar up in Three Lakes the other night—"just trying not to tilt the pinball machine" is the way Steady Eddy puts it—and they got around to discussing the report on snoring that Gene the bartender had found in the "Science Watch" column of the *New York Times.*

"Look at that headline," Gene said. " 'Report Links Snoring to Impaired Thinking.' The story starts: 'Although most people who snore have nothing to worry about, except the annoyance they may cause their bed companions, a University of Florida medical researcher reported last week that in some people this noisy behavior may be associated with impaired thinking.' "

Gene waited for a reaction from his customers, all two of them: the good priest and the good doctor.

"Well," Doc snorted, "as one who has annoyed his share of bed companions over the years, permit me to note that based on personal observation of a particular person, there may indeed be some correlation between snoring and dumbness—er—impaired thinking. Naturally, out of respect for the doctor-patient relationship, which I hold as sacred as others hold the

51

confessional, I would never, *ever* reveal the name—which some have found to be nigh unpronounceable—of this loud, noisy, *impaired* thinker."

The smile on Doc's face was the same one the seventh-grade boys used to have the first time they said a naughty word in front of the Seven-Foot Nun's class at Holy Assumption. There was one big gasp as all the kids sucked in their breath and waited for the ground to open up.

"They were looking the wrong way," Steady Eddy says. "Usually it wasn't the ground opening *up*. It was the sky falling *down*."

They never saw what hit them, the boys would say, sober as judges. It was the hand of God, the Seven-Foot Nun would tell them.

"And once touched by the hand of God," she would remind the breathless class, "one is changed beyond words."

"The doctor," the priest began, "is suggesting, one assumes, that I have been known to snore upon occasion."

"Not upon *occasion*," Doc yelped. "Upon falling *asleep!*"

"Upon occasion," Father Himmelsbach repeated, "and further inference is that he is always the 'observer' watching this 'particular person'—"

"Hearing, I should have said," Doc conceded.

"—and never under observation himself on those occasions without number when I have hauled him out of the stream at day's end—his creel empty, his mouth full of blasphemy—and carried him back to the cabin where he would curse his Maker, ranting and raving, until the rage gradually subsided and one could hear him sleeping the sleep of the damned, his brandy spilling into the inside of his rolled-down waders, dreaming his troubled dreams and making it impossible for anyone else to have any!"

Gene cleared his throat.

"Nice for friends to have things in common," he said. "Nice. Let me get back to this snoring story. We're talking *scientific* here. And I quote: 'In a recent study, A. Jay Block, chief of pulmonary medicine at the university's Health Science Center, found that snoring and low blood-oxygen levels or'— I need a professional opinion here, Doc—"

"Hy-pox-e-mia," Doc said.

" 'Hy-pox-e-mia,' " Gene said, " 'seemed to go hand in hand and both were apparently linked to reduced cognitive skills. Nocturnal hy-pox-e-mia, which affects mostly men, results from breathing lapses in sleep, as many as ten an hour. Tests showed that the resulting oxygen loss impaired general intelligence, starting with concentration, followed by short-term memory and new learning. Dr. Block said people with higher intelligence test scores were less likely to snore than those with lower scores.' "

Gene put the paper down and looked up with the eyes of a true believer.

"Of course," he said, "if you're sleeping alone, snoring is no problem. I would put us in that category, Father."

"I would put *him* in that category more than *you*," Doc said to Gene. "But it's true: witnesses do the snorer in. I remember one time a bunch of us—including our esteemed chaplain here—went up to Canada one September to fish brook trout in a river up above Albany.

"We were in canoes, camped out, the brookies were big as salmon and we had bluebell weather. No bugs. Now guess who the serpent in this paradise was?

"I see by the look in your eye, barkeep, that our shameful secret is safe with you. 'Twas our beloved Himmelsbach. The treachery of this wolf in clergy's clothing! He must have known that he snored from the moment his parents towered over his cradle on that first fateful night they woke up scared sheetless, wondering how a motorcycle had gotten up the stairs and into the nursery. From that moment on, little baby Himmelsbach must have known. But no, he never told us in Canada.

"He slept in a different tent each night those ten days. The other man in the tent would invariably be startled awake, and wind up sleeping out under the canoes. We finally put the demon in a tent by *himself. Ten days!*"

"On the last day," Father Himmelsbach said, "I came out of my tent and everything was gone: People, canoes, tents. I never felt so alone in all my life."

"We came back for him" Doc said. "Hell, he wasn't alone. That snoring had called in every moose north of Nakina. No wonder he's a priest—a wife wouldn't stand for that. God has to."

Gene flew off his stool like a wise old owl and brought out the Chablis.

Hibernating

They were just sitting around in the American Legion Bar up in Three Lakes the other night—"testing the brandy for impurities," as Steady Eddy would say—and they got to talking about the best way to get through a North Country winter.

"The very best way," Gene the bartender said, "is to go away. Someplace where the only ice is in the frozen daiquiris."

He waited for a reaction from his customers, all two of them: the good priest and the good doctor.

"The very best way to get through winter up here," Doc said, "is to be ten years old. Nothing fazes you when you're ten years old. You can get through winter wearing shorts and Adidas."

"The worst way to get through the winter up here," Father Himmelsbach said, "is the way we do it—hauling these old carapaces around like a couple of Galapagos tortoises."

Gene put his elbow on the bar and rested his chin in his hand, because that way his fingers covered up his smile.

"I think what is really the *worst* thing about the winter," Father Himmelsbach said, "is that as you get older, you start worrying about what it can do to you. Like breaking your neck or an arm or a leg. Or both legs.

"When you're a kid, you don't worry about that, about how dangerous just walking on ice is. I remember we used to run full speed in our buckle galoshes and go sliding down every ice patch in town, because you knew that was making all the sidewalks unsafe for the old folks.

"It was your way of getting back at the old folks because— remember, Doc?—it was always the old folks, your father and your mother and your teachers . . . "

"And," Doc interrupted, "your *parish priest.*"

"That's right," Father Himmelsbach said. "All those old folks, those authority figures, always telling you every winter that you shouldn't be sliding on all those ice patches because

54

it was dangerous and that you were gonna fall and kill yourself or at least break something bad, maybe your back. Just wreck your whole life because you were doing a dumb thing like sliding.

"And it was always those same folks who took little-bitty baby steps all winter long, and you watched them looking at their feet in the rubbers, and they were all tense and stiff, and then it came to you like a revelation: The old folks were afraid of falling on the ice and killing themselves or breaking something.

"And when they yelled at all the young kids having fun sliding, they were projecting their fears onto us."

"When you realize how wise our good shepherd is," Doc said to Gene, "you sometimes think he might be in the wrong line of work. He would have made a great barber."

"Or," Gene said into his fingers, "a bartender."

"Now *I* take the little baby steps on the ice," Father Himmelsbach said. "God, I must look like Tim Conway out there."

"We all look like Tim Conway out there," Doc said. "That's why we spend so much time in here."

"It's that wild abandon that you miss," Father Himmelsbach said. "We never thought about falling, and when we *did* fall, we never broke anything, because we always tried to fall on our little keisters, and then the whole gang would be falling down and laughing like idiots, and ice and snow would get ground down right into your corduroy knickers and your seat would be wet right through your long johns. And you all sat down with that little-boy smell, and Sister Agatha would wrinkle her nose and try to teach us something. God, it must have been like being in a room with four dozen wet puppies.

"That's what I miss—that wild, wild abandon. You just throw yourself into it and you don't worry about what could happen to you. You start worrying about what could happen to you and you'd never leave the bedroom."

"Or the barroom," Doc added.

Na roch, Steady Eddy says in moments like this. Your health. Your luck.

"You talk about getting through the winter with wild abandon," Doc said. "Let me tell you about a character who really had abandon. He abandoned *everything* every single winter. His wife. His friends. His business. He just left them all."

"Went to Florida," Gene mumbled.

"Nope," Doc said. "Went to bed. *Hibernated.* For the whole winter. I got this from Jay Keepman. You know—Doc Keepman down in Madison. He says when he was growing up in Watertown, there was a tavernkeeper there—everybody called him Turkey, when Turkey didn't have the present-day connotation. A great guy, Jay said. Had a great business, loved people, loved his wife, loved life, loved everything except the winter in Watertown.

"So every winter, like a bear, Turkey hibernated. He took to his bed and he stayed down all winter long. His wife ran the tavern, took in the money and paid the bills, and Turkey just settled in for a long winter's nap."

"He slept all winter?" Father Himmelsbach asked.

"Well," Doc said, "I don't know how much he slept. But according to Doc Keepman, Turkey was actually in bed all winter long. His wife would bring him food and drink and, presumably, news of the outside world. All through Christmas and New Year's Turkey was in bed—sometimes, I guess, right through Easter. Doc Keepman says that after you got to know Turkey, it didn't seem so strange. What else was there to do in Watertown?"

Behind the bar, Gene's eyes were closed. His head slumped, and he was making the sleeping sounds of a wintering bear.

"All right, Doc," he said, as he sprang to his feet and clapped his hands. "Nice story. House buys a round for Turkey. That's the only jarring note, Doc: 'Turkey' was the wrong name for a smart bird like that."

"*Na roch,*" Doc said.

Words to Live By

They were sitting around the American Legion Bar in Three Lakes the other night—"turning wine into water" is the way Steady Eddy put it—and they got to discussing the Good Old Days in the Chain of Lakes country when the boats were made of wood and the men were made of steel instead of the other way around.

"You know," Gene the bartender said, "those wooden boats required a lot of upkeep. Some of the resort owners spent half the springtime caulking and scraping and painting those rowboats. The new paint was always the same as the old paint. Rowboat green. Then they'd fill 'em full of water so the wood would swell up and the seams would get tight."

Gene waited for a reaction from his other customers.

"Well, sir," Doc said, "I don't think there was ever a better boat for fishing than the roundbottom they used to build down at the old Rhinelander Boat Works. It was quiet as a canoe; you just couldn't beat it for fishing."

"As long as you didn't stand up in it," Father Himmelsbach said.

"That's right," Doc said. "As long as you didn't stand up in it. It could get pretty tippy."

"Especially if you were casting," the priest said. "It seemed like every year you would hear about somebody drowning when they were out fishing, and if there was a survivor, he would always say that he had pleaded with his fishing partner not to stand up to cast, but his partner had stood up anyway and the boat had tipped over and the partner drowned because he couldn't swim."

"That's right," Doc said, "and if they found the boat floating bottom up and there were no survivors, the sheriff would say that probably somebody had stood up in the boat and the boat had tipped over."

"They said that if the boat was a *roundbottom*," Father Himmelsbach said. "If the boat was a *flatbottom*, then they usually said that it was waves or wind or something because a flatbottom was a little more stable and not as tippy as a round-bottom.

"I remember my father standing up in a flatbottom to cast and I got very afraid for us, but the water was like a mirror and nothing happened. I was very relieved when he sat down."

"Like a mirror, hey?" Doc snorted. "I bet every fish within a half-mile saw him standing there."

"I got so indoctrinated," Father Himmelsbach said, "that to this day I have never stood up in a boat except to get in and out when it's tied to the pier. Every fish I have ever caught in a lake I have caught while I was sitting down, and every fish that I have netted for somebody else, I have netted while I was sitting down. You couldn't pay me to stand up in a boat."

Doc looked at Gene the way he does when he's about to set the hook and will need the net in *exactly two minutes.*

"I'll tell you, Father," Doc said, "you stand up there in the pulpit Sunday-in and Sunday-out and that shows me you have a lot more guts than most people."

Behind the bar Gene hunched forward, his chin in his hand, forefinger pressing hard into his upper lip as though to suppress a sneeze.

"You can laugh," Father Himmelsbach said, "but I feel more in control sitting down than standing up."

"You went to Europe and back on a troop ship," Doc said. "Didn't you ever stand up on it?"

"Going over," Father Himmelsbach said, "I was in my bunk. Coming back, I was in my bunk. I stood up when we were tied up at the pier."

They looked at each other and everyone shrugged.

Steady Eddy's contribution to this particular discussion was that it was his experience that most folks who stand in boats are standing up to pee.

"Men folks, that is," he said. "Walleye fishermen do this a lot, I've found, because a lot of their fishing is done in the darkness, and people who would be scandalized if they could see why you were standing up just can't see you."

I thought then of Dynie Mansfield, standing up in all those boats on Little Trout and Constance and Sand and Crab and all the lovely walleye lakes north of Manitowish Waters.

I have never forgotten that time on No Man's Lake with a boat full of walleyes when Dynie very carefully put down his spinning rod, got the coffee can and stood up.

It was a struggle, getting to his feet. He was an old great bear with bum knees and bum legs. When he finally got up, it seemed he just stood there forever, his back to me, the empty coffee can in his left hand. His right hand, even though I couldn't see it, was surely occupied with unzipping and searching. The air was so still you could have heard tinkling if there was tinkling, but there was none. I don't know how many times I cast, retrieved, cast again. Lots. Dynie stood still for so long I got frightened. What if something was wrong and he was about to fall overboard? How would I reach him? How could I pull him in? I was panicky, sensing disaster. I hydroplaned my minnow in.

"Coach," Dynie said right then, looking over his shoulder, "that's the trouble with growing old. You have a hell of a time trying to find it when you need it—and then when you find it you forget what you needed it for."

Words to live by. At the Legion, they still drink to them.

FRIENDS AND FAMILY

I Remember Papa

I got to thinking about the Old Man the other morning. I think about the Old Man on a lot of mornings when I wake up in the darkness before dawn and sense, for a fleeting moment, that I am waking up in his house on the Big Stone Lake and he is standing at the foot of the bed, already fully dressed, his huge hand on my ankle, saying softly: "Time to go."

Then we would go fishing or hunting, and he never mentioned that he was aware I was doing all this on two hours' sleep, having wasted the previous night up in Michigan with Sleepy Ed Stanzil closing all the North Woods bars back to Three Lakes and having sustained one flat tire and two missed turnoffs on the round trip.

I think of the Old Man especially often in October, because it was in October that the Old Man was taken to St. Mary's Hospital in Rhinelander, where he spent the last six months of his life in that iron bed with the side rails, the bed that looked like an oversized baby crib. He died in that thing the following March.

For years, the Old Man and my mother would close up the resort, drain the water out of the pipes, lock up the place and go south for the winter like geese. They usually spent the

61

whole winter in Florida, although they did spend one winter in Arizona, but they never did that again. Sure, it was hot and dry, the Old Man said, but there was no fishing where they were. So the next winter they went back to Florida and they never went to the Southwest again.

"If you play golf," the Old Man said, "go there. But there's no rain there. No fish. Florida kills your sinuses, but nice fishing."

When they first started going to Florida, they waited until after the Christmas season. They would drive down from the North Country, spend the holidays with their kids in Madison and Milwaukee, and then right after New Year's, climb into a Chrysler or a Buick and head for the gulf side of Florida, and all their friends from the Chain of Lakes country were doing the same thing. They had their own little Wisconsin community down there, and everybody still read the *Milwaukee Journal*, the *Vilas County News-Review*, and the *Three Lakes News*.

As they got older and the North Country winters seemed longer, all the folks started going south right after Christmas, then right after Thanksgiving, and finally, most of them took off right after Labor Day.

The Old Man and my mother got it down to October because they had a party of doctors from Ohio who had been coming up for years for the fall muskie fishing, and the Old Man fished with them until his own doctor said it was too hard and exciting to do that every day at his age. So the Old Man and my mother spent a lot of the fall days road-hunting partridge on back roads clear up to the Michigan border.

The Old Man often said that he was just the chauffeur because his partner had gotten so good with her .410 that she was not only getting her share of the birds, she was getting his share too. He was just plain proud of her because she decapitated her birds so cleanly.

"Just shoots their heads off," the Old Man marveled. "You can't do better with a butcher knife."

Sometimes, if the weather wasn't too bad and blowing, they went walleye fishing, and they shared their catch with the Ohio doctors and had a fish fry together and socialized. They then played some poker for low, friendly stakes.

The doctors had fished together all over, including Canada, but they said what they liked best was fishing muskies in

October at Three Lakes. The Old Man felt an obligation to them, so he closed up all the cabins except that one the doctors liked, and he pulled out all the boats for the winter except two for the doctors and the one Alumacraft so he and his hunting partner could go fish walleyes, if she chose.

Then, when the doctors went back to Ohio, the folks closed the resort and started south. Sometimes they left in snow. One time they followed the county plows practically to Antigo. The Old Man said that they liked to leave before the first snow, but they also liked to be back in time for the very last one of the winter.

That last winter he spent in the hospital was a rough winter, a long winter. My mother went to see him every single day, driving early from the Big Stone Lake to Rhinelander and driving back late. On A. That's an isolated road, and when it got bad, the sheriff or one of his deputies would follow her all the way home to make sure she got there safely.

When it got really bad, the nurses at St. Mary's found her an empty room in the hospital and let her spend the night, particularly when it was so bad that even the plows couldn't get out in the city, never mind on "Highway" A.

The Old Man was 78, and everything was going wrong with his body. His heart was bad, he had leukemia and had to be transfused so often it was like pouring oil constantly into an old fish car. The doctor said it was indeed like an old car that had so many miles on it, it was just breaking down all over, and all you could do was just have it sit there and not run it too much. He also said it was like the old days when you put the car up on blocks for the winter, took the wheels off, and just let it sit until spring.

The Old Man never, never complained. When we visited, his wolf's eyes still contained the green fire that Aldo Leopold wrote about, but he knew he was trapped. He knew he was helpless. Then the Old Man fell out of bed and broke his hip. They said it was an accident, and I knew then what the Old Man was trying to do. But it was only the other morning that I realized it was the only thing he ever failed at.

Good News Bible

Cal De Witt smiles a preacher's grin when a friend suggests that he just might be the best Bible salesman in the whole country.

"Well," the UW-Madison professor says, "there's a colleague of mine, David Ehrenfeld, who's a professor at Rutgers. He's been studying the Hebrew Bible, and for the last 10 years I've been studying the Christian. We've come to agree that the Bible, in a real sense, is an ecological handbook on 'How to Live on Earth.'"

De Witt, who has been teaching environmental studies here since 1972, was trained in biology and holds a master's and a Ph.D. from the University of Michigan. Ehrenfeld is a zoologist. Why would two scientists take the Bible so seriously when most scientists now dismiss it as a collection of fables, folklore, and fairy tales? Good literature, many folks say, but bad science.

"Most people's idea of the Bible," DeWitt says, "and this includes scientists, is based on hearsay and not on analysis. A principle of science is to investigate things with rigor and with discipline. Root your understanding in data. Root your understanding in knowledge. Well. Scientists have not studied the Bible in that way. What we have today is a caricature of the Bible. Over the last 10 years I've discovered it's the one book we're not supposed to read!"

To illustrate, De Witt tells of the time he was reading from the "Land Ethic" section of Aldo Leopold's *Sand County Almanac* when a graduate student dropped by the office.

"He asked what was up," DeWitt recalls. "I told him I was just reading Leopold and had reached the point where Leopold was talking about Ezekiel and Isaiah. 'Oh,' said the graduate student. 'I never read those papers.'

"Now, this was a well-versed student," DeWitt laments, "with a degree in the liberal arts, and he thought Ezekiel and Isaiah were modern technical writers! He had no idea they were Hebrew prophets. I think that's an indictment of our educational system."

Still, many who have read the Bible—including ecologists—have given up on it. DeWitt concedes it's often because of the controversial Genesis 128 passage granting man dominion "over the fishes of the sea and the birds of the air." Some people have interpreted that as a veritable license to steal, not to mention poach, trap, and kill everything from the buffalo to the beaver to the beaches of Prince Edward Sound.

DeWitt attributes the wide acceptance of that interpretation to an article written by Lynn White, a University of California professor, in *Science* magazine back in 1967. The article was titled "The Historical Roots of Our Ecological Crisis," and in it White laid the blame for our ecologic crisis squarely on the Judeo-Christian ethic.

"I think his analysis has been extremely helpful," DeWitt says, "in attempting to zero in on the causes of our problems. But White really took all biblical teaching as being represented by that verse. He was saying that teaching was responsible for our ecological crisis, and he concluded that we either had to invent a new religion or adapt the current religion to fit the needs of the present. We had to rethink our old religion."

DeWitt says that's a logical conclusion considering the "reductionist analysis" so long employed by modern science, reducing everything to the smallest pieces possible, be it bones, tissue, atoms, sub-atoms—or a single passage from the Bible. The only way to get the Bible's ecological message, DeWitt advises, is to read all the passages in the Bible and read the entire Bible over and over and over again.

After 10 years, Dewitt says he is astounded by the ecological principles he now finds and understands in the Bible, which he has in its totality indexed and cross-referenced on a computer program. Not specific solutions to specific problems, at least not yet, he says with a grin. But principles. The Bible is stuffed full as a milkweed pod with ecological principles.

"If you look at that classic passage on dominion by inself," DeWitt says, "and if you look at nothing else, it does seem to be a very, very domineering dominion. But if you then read that through in context, you see it quite differently."

As an example, he cites a blessing from the early chapters of Genesis: Be fruitful and multiply and replenish the earth. This, he notes, is frequently used as justification for unlimited human population growth.

"But," DeWitt argues, "if you look at this in context, you find that the fish of the sea and the birds of the air also have this responsibility to be fruitful and multiply and replenish the earth."

Now, knowing that, Dewitt continues, if you then look at the concept of dominion over the fish of the seas and the birds of the air—and if you do that in *obedience* to the biblical teachings—that "dominion" means you must allow the blessing "be fruitful and multiply" to apply to the fish of the sea and the birds of the air, too. When we allow that, DeWitt says, we cross the line from harsh dominion to stewardship.

"It's quite apparent," he insists. "If they are to multiply, that means you don't cut down the trees and you don't fill in the marshes. There is a great deal of teaching that seriously warns against destroying the fruitfulness of the Creation. Which, of course, is what we're doing."

Well, not everyone is destroying, DeWitt admits. He has some farmer friends up in Canada who practice what the Bible preaches, including keeping the Sabbath.

The Sabbath, of course, is a day of rest for people—Christian, Jewish or just plain Packers fans. But DeWitt says that in Exodus 23, which is part of the first five books of the Old Testament (referred to in Judaism as the Torah), there is a prescription for a Sabbath for the land. Leviticus 25 and 26 also prescribe a Sabbath for the land.

"The teaching," DeWitt says, "is that the land itself must be given its times to recuperate, to restore itself, even to enjoy itself for itself without being pressed by us to produce.

"This Sabbath for the land is not one day out of a week. This is one year out of every seven years. For agricultural land, this is the time for lying fallow."

DeWitt's Canadian friends farm up on the 52nd parallel in Alberta. They grow barley, and it's only a 65-day growing season. They give the land a Sabbath every second year. They're a Reformed Protestant community, and they, like Amish and Mennonite farmers—who rest their fields every seven years—do it because the Bible teaches a Sabbath for the land.

In the biblical teaching, DeWitt points out, "the land" means everything. The land is a piece, a part of the whole of creation. Statements in Leviticus and Exodus say that this is so that the animals, too, will have food to eat, as well as the poor and the hungry.

"In other words," DeWitt says, "if it's cropland you have or a vineyard, you're supposed to allow your whole vineyard to be available—to the poor, to the hungry and to all the creatures. Much of what we are doing today in ecology—particularly in the new field called 'restoration ecology'—is thoroughly consistent with this concept."

As a matter of fact, DeWitt adds, many of the old respected environmental organizations—the Sierra Club, the Audubon Society, the Nature Conservancy—all have their roots in Judeo-Christian teachings. Dewitt claims that he is following in the footsteps of John Muir, Aldo Leopold, and others who have their roots there, too. Wendell Berry, Dewitt reports mischievously, paraphrases the Bible all the time, but no one realizes, "because no one reads the Bible."

The Bible teachings lead to the inescapable conclusion, DeWitt says, that the universe is not only well ordered but that it is just. Justice prevails. Why is it well ordered? Why is it just? It is only when you spend time in the natural world that you begin to understand why, that you begin to see the interconnectedness of the entire universe. That's the reason Dewitt loves to take his students outside. "It shocks some people," he says, "when I tell them Christ did all his teaching on field trips."

Trout Shangri-La

There is a magical place somewhere south of Ishpeming in Michigan's Upper Peninsula where John Voelker owns some wild land and among his tenants—none of whom pays rent—are wild brook trout. The trout have a symbiotic relationship with the landlord. Without one, the other would be hard-pressed to survive.

Voelker owns 160 acres of wilderness surrounding the fabled (among anglers) Frenchman's Pond. For this retired jurist and author, the land is a refuge from too much civilization. It is also under siege by too much civilization.

In September of 1987, the *Milwaukee Journal* sent photographer Brent Nicastro and me up to inteview the Grand Old Master.

Voelker takes us out to Frenchman's Pond in his white Jeep Cherokee, going slowly, almost hugging the highway shoulder so all the traffic passes us. The back of the Jeep is stuffed to overflowing with all the trout gear that money could buy.

As he guides his jeep down the bumpy dirt tracks toward Shangri-La, we emerge where a logging operation has been clear-cutting right to where its property ends and Voelker's begins.

He doesn't say the vandals are at his very gates now. The logging operations, he says, do provide work for men who have less and less of it these days in these parts.

We leave the barren lands and enter Voelker country, not far from Lake Superior, maybe 15 miles or so, in his beloved Marquette County.

There is the forest, dark, mysterious and alive. A number of weathered wooden signs scream silent warnings to trespassers. One faded sign in particular catches photographer Brent Nicastro's eye. It reads "Home of the UP Cribbage Champ."

"I'm impressed," Brent says.

Brent lives in Madison but has a cabin up on the Sturgeon River backwaters in the Upper Peninsula, near Iron Mountain. When they're up in Michigan, to hear Brent tell it, all he and his wife, Nora, do is play cribbage.

"This is one of the few places left like this," our host says as the jeep crawls through trees that brush and touch roof, hood, and fenders. "It's a jungle, a northern jungle. It's also one of the few places around here that holds wild brook trout because the water's ice cold in here."

He shifts into neutral and the jeep growls like a leashed animal. We roll past an open spot strewn with apples he has put out for his tenants.

"You put apples out for the deer?" I ask.

"I'd like to preserve this," he confides, "not only for the fish, but for the beautiful trees we've been driving through. I know there are places that you can give your land to and I suppose I could do that and get a team of lawyers to draw up a 104-page will that says; 'DO NOT CUT TREES! and DO NOT DO THIS! and DO NOT DO THAT!'

"But I have two grandsons and they just love it up here. They've been coming up since they were kids and now they're grown. One's still in college. I've sworn them to try and save this place. With tears in their eyes, they have vowed to save the trees and the fish. End of statement."

The jeep fords a trickle of water, straining for a toehold on the sloping rock outcropping.

"Oooh," Voelker says. "Look at what the bear did. LOOK at what the bear DID! That's a sugar plum bush. There's still a few bears around here. That bush was bending over before and now some bear just pulled it all down."

He seems pleased about that.

John Voelker is more than a lawyer; he's a legend in Upper Michigan. He graduated from the University of Michigan, served as prosecuting attorney for Marquette County and sat "for a spell" as a justice on the Michigan Supreme Court.

In addition to writing 100 legal decisions in the three years he served, he also wrote books under the pen name Robert Traver, a practice he had started while a prosecutor. He used his mother's maiden name, figuring "the taxpayers might have thought it improper if the DA used his own."

He left the court to write books and fish trout full time. He has kept track of the books: 11. He has not kept track of the trout, most of which are released to fight another day and another year.

As an author, he is particularly proud of the books *Trout Magic* and *Trout Madness,* which have become classics in the literature of fly fishing. But it was his fourth book, the best-selling *Anatomy of a Murder,* that brought him fame, fortune, and the leisure to enjoy his beloved Frenchman's Pond as often as he wants, which is every day of the season.

Anatomy was a Book of the Month Club selection and was made into a motion picture by Otto Preminger. The 1959 movie starred James Stewart, George C. Scott, Eve Arden, Ben Gazzara, and Lee Remick, with an original score composed and performed by Duke Ellington.

The picture was shot on location in Voelker country, and it just may have been the biggest happening to come into the Upper Peninsula since the grayling (a cousin of the salmon) left. In the movie, Jimmy Stewart loved trout fishing, Italian cigars and jazz records just as John Voelker did in real life.

The legend has given up his Italian cigars since those palmy days, but he hasn't given up much else.

At the end of the trail, we park and walk down to one of the most famous fish camps on the planet, the storied shack overlooking the storied beaver flowage called Frenchman's Pond.

The pond surface is undimpled at the moment; not a single rise puddles the water, yet you sense that the brook trout hiding in the depths know that the landlord is back on the premises.

Voelker has a fine house, an elegant house in town, but this is where he truly lives, in the company of old friends who share his passions for chasing mushrooms and berries and trout—especially trout—in the enchanting country where he was a boy.

One of those friends is Charles Kuralt of CBS-TV, who said last summer that in all the many years of doing his "On the Road" interviews, the greatest character, indeed "the greatest man," he ever met was John Voelker.

"I think I got Charles Kuralt interested in fly fishing," Voelker allows.

Voelker lived in Chicago for three years, working for "a high-powered law firm," but he couldn't take the city.

"A trout couldn't live there," he laments, "and neither could I."

So he returned to his native heath and settled into the Upper Peninsula for life. The finest catch he made in Illinois, he boasts, was his wife, Grace.

"I took her out of Oak Park," he says, smiling.

Voelker asks if I want to borrow a fly rod and I say no, I just want to watch him. He shrugs, takes a seat on a casting platform and holds court. He puts on a demonstration worthy of a sports show, Big John Wayne with a lariat. Yet he's not showing off; he's fly fishing.

I ask for a roll cast and he sends that vertical magic circle of fly line rolling across the surface like a hula hoop. I want to applaud. The Old Master is playing his violin in front of the fiddlers.

Here is a man in his eighties who still has the arm, the coordination, the control of a Roger Clemens nicking the corners of home plate.

"What really converted me to fly fishing," he says, "was that I learned it's possible to catch a fish and put it back. You can't do that if you shoot the fish."

It's his way of telling you that he never followed in the footsteps of his father, who was "a bang-bang" deer hunter.

"He hunted with an old .44 Winchester lever action," Voelker recalls, "and he must have shot hundreds of deer with it. All my brothers shot their deer with it, too.

"I own the gun now, but I have yet to shoot my first deer with it."

But in the old days, Voelker admits, he did hunt because his friends did. Voelker hunted partridge until his partridge-hunting friends began dying. Then the very last one died.

"The first time I went hunting after his funeral," Voelker remembers, "I was driving along and saw three partridge sitting on the roadside. I poked my gun out the window—that $500 Remington over-and-under shotgun—and fired it straight up in the air! That was the parting shot of my hunting career.

"Like most of the others, it didn't hurt anything."

The flyfishing this day doesn't hurt anything, either. A cold drizzle begins to fall and we repair to the cluttered shack for bourbon in a cup and a hand of cribbage between the Upper Peninsula champ and the presumptuous photographer challenger from the south.

"It was his suggestion that we play for money," Brent swears later. "Well, I beat him the first game for a quarter."

There is a break in the rain and they go back outside for more photography.

When they return, Brent skunks the old pro and so wins double: 50 cents. The third game is closer and Brent has a sweep and a dollar bill from the UP Cribbage Champ.

Voelker is as gracious about losing at cribbage as he is about not catching any trout. Sometimes, that's just the way it goes. Fishermen get philosophical about their losses. Book writers, too.

"I've written 11 published books," Voelker replies when I inquire if he is writing anything now, "and I'm not planning to write another one.

"I say that's enough for one guy for a while, you know, for this incarnation."

He says he doesn't know if the writing takes too much energy out of him or what.

"I keep notes of stories I'm going to write," he says, "but it's always next week that I'm going to write them. After fishing season. After football season. After Christmas. After I finish reading these essays I'm reading by Ralph Ellison. After.

"I think the simplest explanation is that now I'm genuine old—and I'm running out of steam. You know, I've never been this old before. I'm 84, born around the turn of the century, although of later years, sometimes I get turned around about precisely which century.

"I might take a try at some nonfishing essays. After all, there are only so many things you can say about fishing—either you catch some or you don't and variants of that."

Sure, your honor, I think. But you already have said things about fishing that no one has ever said better because it simply cannot be said better.

In the preface to the book *Trout Magic*, Robert Traver wrote the classic *Testament of a Fisherman* and broke the heart of every fishing writer on the planet.

"I fish," Traver-Voelker wrote, "because I love to; because I love the environs where trout are found, which are invariably beautiful, and hate the environs where crowds of people are found, which are invariably ugly;

"Because of all the television commercials, cocktail parties and assorted social posturing I thus escape; because, in a world where most men seem to spend their lives doing things they hate, my fishing is at once an endless source of delight and an act of small rebellion; because trout do not lie or cheat and cannot be bought or bribed or impressed by power, but respond only to quietude and humility and endless patience;

"Because I suspect that men are going along this way for the last time, and I for one don't want to waste the trip; because mercifully there are no telephones on trout waters; because only in the woods can I find solitude without loneliness; because bourbon out of an old tin cup always tastes better out there;

"Because maybe one day I will catch a mermaid; and, finally, not because I regard fishing as being so terribly important but because I suspect that so many of the other concerns of men are equally unimportant—and not nearly so much fun."

John Voelker died in Negaunee County on March 18 at age 87.

He was found dead in his car. Witnesses said he was slumped over the wheel even before the car rolled into a snowbank. Police think it was a heart attack.

A lot of trout fisherfolk, especially the ones who can read, cried when they heard.

"I got lucky," Brent says. "I'm saving the same dollar so we can play for it the next time I see him. He's still The Champ and that sign can sure stay up."

OLD CROWS

Nothing to Crow About

A ny time the conversation turns to Old Crow, you're bound to get an opinion from the good old boys at the bait shop.

"Of course," Steady Eddy concedes, "Wild Turkey is a pretty good ice-breaker too."

The subject of Old Crow came up the other day. Specifically, the subject of the crow that was killed by a Fond du Lac man last October and confiscated by the U.S. Fish and Wildlife Service. The dead bird was a white crow.

"You ever see a white crow?" the Indian asked the assemblage.

"Only him," Steady Eddy said, pointing to your agent the way a beagle points to a found-out rabbit.

"Well, the raven is a magical bird," said the Indian, "and the crow is just the raven's smaller cousin—we call him the 'white man's raven'—so the crow is magical too. You know no Indian is going to shoot one. Especially a white crow."

"Here we go with the sermonette," Steady said.

"Look," the Indian said, "you got a white crow flying around out there with a bunch of black crows. The Old Ones could make a whole religion out of that. They could tell you stories until your eyes got big as a horned owl's. But not one of the Old Ones would have killed that white crow just to have it stuffed and mounted by a taxidermist—and would you hazard a guess as to what color the taxidermist was?"

"Do you think you have a problem?" Steady asked the Indian.

"I have a problem with anybody who shoots or stuffs a crow, especially a white crow," the Indian replied. "I mean, if the guy's out there starving, fine, then that's a whole different thing. As they say up on the Hill, you have different parameters then.

"But this guy wasn't starving to death. I mean, who the hell is going to be starving to death on the east side of Fond du Lac? Come on. The guy killed the white crow because it's special, it's rare."

"That's probably right," Steady Eddy said. "The paper says here that the hunter who killed the crow said he did it for his 'personal collection.' He killed the white crow, took it to the taxidermist and it was just waiting its turn when a story about the white crow came out in the Sunday edition of the *Fond du Lac Reporter*. Then it makes the Associated Press wire, and the feathers hit the fan."

"The paper also said that the white crow had attracted the attention of birdwatchers for more than a year, and they reported that it was often seen flying in a flock of five or six other crows that were black," said the Indian. "Maybe those birdwatchers got curious about what happened to that white crow and tracked it down to that hunter and then to that taxidermist."

"Or maybe," Steady said, "to the taxidermist first and then to that hunter second. Don't monkey with the little old ladies in tennis shoes. Or the little old men."

"How did that hunter expect to keep it a secret?" the Indian said. "How many mounted white crows are there in Fond du Lac?"

"The feds got into it," Steady said, "because federal regulations prohibit the hunting of birds such as crows—white or black—for sport. They may be killed only if they're deemed a 'nuisance' or 'a threat to public health' or if they are causing 'crop damage.'

"Now, Wisconsin hunting regulations say 'crows, grackles, red-winged blackbirds and cowbirds may be killed at any time without permit, when causing damage or about to cause damage to trees, crops, livestock or wildlife, or when concentrated in large numbers that may cause a nuisance.' "

"You know," the Indian said, "that guy who shot the crow is 27 and still undeveloped. If I was the judge, I wouldn't put him in jail or anything. I would just take his gun away until he had memorized this from the Sioux:

At night may I roam
Against the winds may I roam
At night may I roam
When the owl is hooting
May I roam.
At dawn may I roam
Against the winds may I roam
At dawn may I roam
When the crow is calling
May I roam.

"Then I would have him memorize what the Cheyenne said about the crow: 'He has renewed our life. He has taken pity on us.' I would also give the hunter his gun back when he gave the white crow its life back."

Crow Consciousness

"The crow," John Burroughs once wrote, "always has the walk and air of a lord of the soil."

The old naturalist had it right. The great birds have the dignity you associate with hawks or eagles or other travelers of the high places who always seem to be less earthbound and mundane.

"The crow," Steady Eddy says, "has the dignity of a mortician, and that figures, because they're both in the same line of work."

The old Steady has it right, too.

We, most of us, don't like to think about practical cleanup work that this carbon cycle requires, and that's why, Steady insists, worms and hyenas and turkey vultures don't get to be school mascots.

"It's not your average line of work," Steady observes, "but someone's got to do it. We can't all be parakeets."

After a lifetime of crow-watching, I didn't really appreciate them fully until one ice-fishing season when I watched them far out on the ice, settling down on the surface and walking stiffly around the frozen, abandoned bodies of dead fish.

One eventually comes to respect the scavengers, I wrote— once the brandy began to unclog my arterial system. They go about their work with an almost ritualistic dignity. They are professional and correct, calculating the logistics of disposing of the dead thing before them. And then they proceed to pick out its eyes.

In recent days, my crow-consciousness has been raised by walks in the Gallistel woods.

Hundreds and hundreds of crows skim the treetops in the late afternoons, each aware of the alien who trudges heavily through their domain, each aware of the alien's singularity and of their teeming superiority.

Even the cries of their sentinels seem casual and not strident; urgent alarms are unneeded in the great swirling mass of a conquering army. It's like some historic link-up, a meeting of the Russians and the Americans on the Elbe, a babbling of joy and triumph and hardship shared.

And it takes place every afternoon.

"To a crow," Steady notes, "another crow is a sight for sore eyes. Every day."

John Burroughs says the same thing. One morning the old naturalist put some fresh meat out on the snow near his study window. Presently a crow came and carried it off, alighting with it upon the ground in the vineyard.

"While he was eating of it," Burroughs reported, "another crow came, and alighting a few yards away, slowly walked up to this fellow and stopped."

Burroughs admits that, at this point, he fully expected to see—as would have been the case with domestic fowl or animals—a struggle over the food.

"Nothing of the kind," he relates, and you can almost hear his surprise. "The feeding crow stopped eating, regarded the other for a moment, made a gesture or two, and flew away. Then the second crow went up to the food and proceeded to take his share. Presently, the first crow came back, each seized a portion of the food and flew away with it. Their mutual respect and goodwill seemed perfect."

As to whether it was really so in our human sense, or simply an illustration of the instinct of mutual support that seems to prevail among gregarious birds, Burroughs throws up his hands.

"I know not," he says.

What he does know is that birds that are solitary in their habits, like hawks or woodpeckers, behave quite differently toward each other in the presence of their food.

"The crow," John Burroughs observes, "has fine manners."

I watch crows soar over Gallistel woods and I remember the times I shot at them in the old days, and I wonder if they know I did that.

"I think they know," Hugh Percy says. "When the carcass is barely cold and the birds show up, how are you gonna keep secrets?"

Augie Derleth, who walked among crows as much as anyone, loved their cawing and insisted that it was a sound as wild as the shrilling of loons or the squeaky-hinge calling of eagles.

Here, Augie recorded, is a voice of one who has resisted all the blandishments of civilization, who has defied the best efforts of man to tame or to slay him. It is curious to reflect that the crow's voice should comfort a man in his solitude, however much the crow's rascality be known; yet it is so.

It is as if this proof of the essential wildness of this black scavenger was an immutable assurance of the persistence of the wilderness, of the continuity of life itself. For there is never any dearth of crows—they survive every season, they escape the most dedicated hunter, they return as inevitably as the seasons themselves.

Winter is particularly the crow's season, Augie noted. However difficult the foraging, he seems in this season to come into his own, hurling his challenge from every corner of the gray winter sky, out and about in all manner of weather.

"They're on the increase," Steady says, "along with rats and roaches. If they could count the way they multiply . . . "

"Maybe they can't count," Perce said. "But I think they got it figured."

Gathering of Crows

They come every afternon now to the winter-stripped oak woods behind the house.

Crows.

Hundreds and hundreds of them from all points of the compass. Raucous. Wheeling. Windblown. Careening. Soaring like cinders, settling like stones.

The great black birds are drawn to this Stonehenge of a place even as the Druids have always been drawn to the Magical Circle.

It is awesome to see so many of the glistening scavengers assembled together. Hundreds of them, talking all at once, exchange the day's intelligence—the small talk and the large lessons. Then only a few talking, synthesize the experiences into bite-size chunks the troops can handle. Then no birds talking at all, save the air-traffic controllers dispatching in impressive, constant flights the manageable squadrons that melt away the chaotic mass.

The crows leave this staging area silent—total eerie silence.

I don't know what the crows talk about in their conclaves—their daily conferences—but they seem to be thriving, and they seem to be on the increase.

As they settle into the naked trees in the freezing twilight, I think of Jurgen Herbst recalling his boyhood in Germany, "when the east wind blew across the plains and the crows came back to town."

"Nietzsche knew that too," Jurgen observed, "and he wrote a poem to remind us. I send you a copy and add my own translation. . . ."

The poem was titled "Vereinsamt"—"Deserted":

Cawing crows,
their wings awhir, are moving towards town.
Soon it will snow—
Blessed he who still lives in his home.

Now you stand still,
look backward, aye, for oh so long!
What made you fool
winters ago, escape into the world?

The world—a gate
to a thousand deserts, mute and cold.
Whoever lost
What you have lost, will stop nowhere.

Now you stand tall,
to wintry wanderings condemned
like smoke
that always stretches towards colder skies.

Flee, bird, and croak
your desert-bird lament!
And hide, you fool,
your bleeding heart in ice and scorn!

Cawing crows,
their wings awhir, are moving towards town.

Soon it will snow—
Cursed he who does not have a home.

With the words of Nietzsche in your eyes and the cries of crows in your ears, the images pinwheel in the mind's eye like a kaleidoscpoe twirled in front of the Christmas tree:

•There is Lillian Lawson's English class at West Allis Central, docile as pigeons, listening to a voice that could belong to Poe himself, yet seemingly belonging to the gentle teacher. A voice perching above us all like some great terrifying knowledge.

•There is the Chippewa from Minnesota, Gerald Vizenor, blowing on his fingertips and recalling:

"Seven woodland crows stayed all winter this year among the white earth trees . . . tribal land all wire marked . . . fox runs under rusting plows . . . seven woodland crows stayed all winter this year marking the dead landmen who ran the woodland out of breath. . . ."

Loren Eiseley writes of falling asleep at a pond's edge once and waking to find a mature heron poised over him:

"It was certain that momentarily he did not recognize me for a man. Perhaps he was merely curious. Perhaps it was only my little brown eye in the mud that he wanted. As this thought penetrated my sleeping brain, I rolled, quick as a frog shrieking underfoot, into the water. The great bird, probably as startled as I, rose and beat steadily off into the wind, his long legs folded gracefully behind him."

Perhaps that is the uneasiness we have in the presence of crows and ravens and the burial birds. They, too, wait for our eyes. And yet, in the same instant, we know intuitively that Robert Frost was right when he said:

> *The way a crow*
> *Shook down on me*
> *The dust of snow*
> *From a hemlock tree*
> *Has given my heart*
> *A change of mood*
> *And saved some part*
> *Of a day I had rued.*

Born Survivors

You have to admire crows, Steady Eddy says, because while they're not the only ones out on the ice these days, they are the only ones who are out there barefoot.

When we were kids, I always associated crows with the "crowbites" that Charlie Kaiser at Holy Assumption school was always finger-flicking into our unsuspecting seventh-grade noggins when we were standing in line waiting to go to Mass or to confession or to the boys' john.

A good crowbite could hurt so much it might draw tears. It always did draw a sharp cry that you tried to choke back so the Seven-Foot Nun didn't hear and start sweeping toward the sound like a Great Horned owl homing in on a nest of field mice who are used to sleeping with one eye open.

Later, in the snow-filled sand pit up at the Big Stone Lake—in the olden days when it was legal to dump garbage there—we stalked the crows and ravens with our scoped .22.

In the white sheets, we fancied ourselves Finnish ski troopers fooling the Russian bear. But we didn't fool the North Country bird.

Crows, you learn quickly, are born *survivors*, and maybe that's why you have to admire them. Whether they're walking around the ice fields in search of fish eyes or sitting atop a light pole at the Red Owl, this is a bird of another feather altogether.

"Crows are funny when they walk," Steady Eddy says, "and they're funny when they talk but when they're just sitting there silent as stones with the beady eyes on *you*, we're talking spook time."

It's awesome to see crows in the North Country winter, hundreds and hundreds of them glistening in the icy afternoons, flying in from all points of the compass, rackety and wheeling and windblown, settling into the bare branches of trees picked clean as animal bones in the North Country snows.

It all seems so random and disorganized. Then, as you watch them with your own beady eye for a spell, it comes into your head eventually, with a shock—"just like a crow bite," Steady Eddy says—that what you're seeing is not random or disorganized at all.

Crows *know* what they're doing when they assemble this way. They're exchanging information about the day's pickings and proceedings just like pilots newly arrived from a thousand all-day cross-country flights.

You can *sense* that they're talking of grid coordinates and landmarks and weather systems AND the precise locations of all those big and little carcasses in the snow.

That's not the spooky part for me. The spooky part is when they all *stop* talking. *All of them.* One moment, hundreds of birds are chattering, clattering away, and the very next moment: *Absolute stillness.* It's like watching a waterfall with the sound turned off.

Then, like planes leaving an airport, they depart by twos and threes, *silently* as gliders or hawks on the thermal. They're leaving these precincts for the night's roosting place, the little town's cemetery woods where there is no living man to endanger their sleep. It is no wonder we called our spy planes "blackbirds."

One moment the skeleton trees are full of birds, a forest of surreal Christmas trees dangling with ornaments, and in the very next instant every single one has fled, every single ornament is gone. The whole flock has vanished—a million feathers making no more sound than one.

Not many people would describe the crow as "exotic"; indeed, many old timers still consider it a "varmint" as the oldtimey outdoors magazines used to call it—and some of the newtimey magazines, too.

Sure, it's hard to love birds like these unless you put your mind to it. They glory in our garbage, grow strong on our leavings. Picking through our wastes, they know us as well as the rats and the roaches know us. Steady Eddy says we're talking "street-smarts."

Crows are survivors and their numbers are increasing. And there is a moral for us in that. You watch crows settle themselves in the winter twilight and they seem as carefree now as they seem on a midsummer's day: They can survive outside by their wits and their eyes in the bitterest of winters. They do this without tools or snowmobile suits or Sorel boots or blackberry brandy. Naked as jaybirds, they are so free of fear out there that I shiver for us because despite all our high-tech stuff, those tough old birds, like the tough old rats and the tough old roaches, are going to survive us. Give them credit.

Just now I remember the words of Ramona Wilson, a Colville Indian from Nespelem, Washington, which appeared in the Native American anthology *Voice of the Rainbow*.

> *Once we dreamed of eagles,*
> *the scurrying flights, of black bears,*
> *beckoning tails of deer*
> *white in the darkness of noon woods;*
> *but we see instead the road's dust*
> *rising slowly into the dead sky*
> *has smothered and discolored all that*
> *lies beside.*
> *The chicken hawks wheel far small.*
> *We are grateful for them.*
> *Fat, cold-eyed crows lighten our day.*

We keep wrinkling up our noses at the scavengers and, all the time we're scorning them, we keep creating more waste so more scavengers are needed to keep up with us. Is that why

we picked the bald eagle, a scavenger, to be our national symbol? Maybe, Steady Eddy says, when we didn't know what we
were doing, we knew what we were doing.

HUNTING

Coming of Age

Connie sat there on the old jack-pine stump that had been his personal deer stand for the last 25 years and talked to himself the way old hunters who are also old grandpas do.

"This will be the worst damn deer hunt you have ever been on, Conrad. You will be in pure hell before this day is over and you've got nobody to blame but yourself because you brought it on."

He shifted the rifle in his lap and peered at the fringe of the cedar swamp in which, at this very moment, Bill and the grandsons were slithering and stumbling in their misbegotten attempts to get old Grandpa a shot at a deer.

The cedar swamp was as serene as church. To Connie, it always looked like those autumnal scenes of the leafless Wisconsin woods that Mel Kishner used to paint for the Sunday *Milwaukee Journal* at the beginning of deer season.

The quiet in the swamp meant that Bill and the boys probably hadn't started their drive yet. Most likely because they wanted to make sure that Grandpa was in place on his stump— all settled in, his breathing back to normal after the long trek from the cabin, his gun loaded and ready.

They probably were figuring in enough time for Grandpa to have a coffee out of the thermos to get him sensitized and alert for the trophy buck they promised to flush out for him.

"You got to be really wired today, Grandpa," Chuckie had warned him as he poured the breakfast coffee. "You're gonna see more deer than you saw in the last five years. We're talking Action City!"

Connie didn't feel a need to pour anything out of the thermos. He didn't need to get himself 'wired.' God, just to be out here, sitting on a stump and just breathing that crisp air of the country, was excitement enough. Of course, how the hell could you explain that to somebody half your age, as Bill was, or somebody from a different planet altogether, as Bill's boys were?

It was something he couldn't talk about because nobody in the deer camp was his age.

"Say it," he said to himself. "Nobody here is as old as you are and how can you expect anybody younger to understand what the hell's happening to you?"

What was happening to him he really didn't understand himself. It had started happening three, four deer seasons back and he hadn't told anybody about it until he had told Doc just this last summer.

Doc had never been much of a hunter, not deer or birds or anything. He fished trout and that was pretty much it. But Doc was never judgmental about hunters, and you could talk to Doc about the serious stuff like growing old and life and death because that's what Doc dealt with all the time. Plus, and it was a big plus, Doc and Connie were the same age and had gone through a lot of the same stuff together like school and the Army and arthritis.

"It's hard to share bladder problems with the teenie-boppers," Doc said.

Connie just knew that he was going to share his problem with Doc because he had to share it with someone and who else was there? Some way, somehow he would find a way to just bring it into the conversation and share it. He really felt like he was going through a change of life or something.

It was at Connie's birthday party last summer that the opportunity arose. They were in the back yard having brats and beer and a birthday cake with one candle. It was a tradition since Connie had turned 60, some seasons back.

"Makes sense," Doc said. "After all, you're only celebrating this birthday today. You've already celebrated the rest. Who the hell needs a forest fire?"

It was the present from Bill and the grandsons that did Connie in. Everybody raved about the thoughtfulness and the originality. It was a birthday card with a magnificent deer in watercolors.

"Grandpa," the card read. "This card entitles you to the best deer hunt of your life this season. We will drive the cedar swamp until you get THE FIRST DEER THIS YEAR. PERIOD. Happy Birthday from 'the Swamp Rats.' "

It was signed by his four grandsons and Bill.

That's when Conrad cornered Doc for a talk.

"Well," Doc said. "It's easy to see where they got their genes. You must be touched and I am impressed. They're saying that Grandpa gets his deer before anybody gets a deer. They love their Grandpa. Not too shabby, Conrad."

"They're doing it," Connie said, "because Grandpa didn't get a deer the last couple of seasons."

"So, this year," Doc said, "they're making sure Grandpa gets his deer. Grandpa doesn't like that?"

"Doc," Connie said, "I've been going out there and just sitting on my stump and I really don't care if I never shoot another deer in my life."

Connie sat as silent as a partridge for a spell.

"The reason I didn't get a deer the last four seasons," he said finally, "is that I've been sitting there with an empty gun."

The look on Doc's face hadn't been there since the time he hooked an owl on his back cast.

"An empty gun?"

"That's right," Connie said. "An empty gun. Unloaded. I knew I wasn't going to shoot it so why the hell should I load it?"

"You know," Doc said, "that's like fishing without a hook. That's really pretty funny, Conrad."

"Actually," Connie said, "the first two seasons I loaded the gun, I even shot it in the air to fool them. Then, of course, I had to clean the damn gun and I thought, 'Boy, how dumb can you get?' "

"Conrad, Conrad," Doc said gently. "And you bought the licenses and the deer tags and everything."

"I'll tell you, Doc," Connie said. "Don't think I haven't felt like a damn fool out there. Deer are going by you like cows going to the barn and you have to pretend—you have to lie—about not seeing any deer or not having a good clear shot available.

"Why couldn't I just come right out and tell them that it was just getting hard for me to kill anymore and all I wanted to do was just sit on my stump and watch the world go by? But if I sat out there without a gun in deer season, you know they'd think Grandpa had gone soft or senile or something.

"Grandpa raised them all to hunt and what happens if hunting isn't important to Grandpa anymore?"

"You can't tell Bill?"

"What the hell could I say? Especially after all this time. I just put it off and put it off and got by and all of a sudden you just can't put it off anymore."

"Like a trip to the doctor," Doc said.

"It's just got harder for me to kill," Connie said. "That's what it really is—and I was ashamed to tell anybody about it. Isn't that terrible? My own family."

Doc didn't really answer until about a week later. He mailed Connie a photocopy of some pages from *Wisconsin Trails* magazine. There was a handwritten note in Doc's prescription scrawl:

"We were straightening up our magazine selection in the waiting room and thought this applied to your case. Mel Ellis, as you probably know, was an outdoor writer for the *Milwaukee Journal* before he turned legit and wrote books. This is from an interview circa 1971. Take two aspirin and call me in the morning."

Connie smiled and read. It was like hearing a friend talk to him over a coffee.

"It's getting tough for me to kill," Mel Ellis had said back in 1971. "I've got a theory that eventually no one will shoot anything or kill anything. It's just a matter of becoming civilized."

Connie knew now that Mel Ellis' words had gotten to him. Connie liked to think that they got to him in the same way a grain of sand gets to an oyster and the oyster then forms a pearl around that grain.

He felt the sun toasting his cheeks. He inhaled the still, chill air, cold as trout water. He poured a half cup from the steaming thermos and waited.

The first deer materialized in the swamp fringe. The rack on its head was as big as an elk's. It stood still, ears flicking, listening. It trotted toward him casually, never seeing him.

"Hello," Connie said, and the deer just exploded straight up in the air, it looked like ten feet, and bounded past him like a kangaroo. Connie thought he saw fear in the deer's eyes. Then again, it might have been only disbelief.

He could hear yells and shouting coming from the swamp and suddenly deer began appearing like apparitions. One here. One there. Two. Three at a time. God, Connie thought. It was like watching a colony of field mice being flushed by the barn cats.

What a drive his boys were putting on in that jungle. He knew what it took out of you to drive like that and he was washed in guilt because they were doing it for him. Getting Grandpa a deer that Grandpa didn't want to shoot.

But he was so damn proud of them because they were doing something for somebody else, sweating and falling down and getting wet and scratched and he hoped that they at least saw some of the magnificent animals moving like shadows away from them.

Connie sat there, sipping his coffee and marveling at the show the boys had provided. I should have filmed it, he thought. Yeah, that's all you need, he told himself. So they could see the deer coming out of the swamp like rabbits and nobody shooting.

Maybe somebody would shoot Grandpa and they could film that.

The deer all disappeared to the north. By late afternoon, those that hadn't been shot would have doubled back to bed down in the cedar for another night.

It was almost ten minutes before the next apparition came out of the swamp. It was Bill. He stood still, breathing deeply, his eyes seeking his father, surveying the area around the stump, looking for a downed deer, a blood trail, something.

Then, he walked slowly up the rise to Connie, his eyes watching the ground all the way, seeing the deep tracks in the soft soil.

"I didn't hear any shots from you," Bill said. "They must have come through here like rabbits."

He hunkered down at Connie's knees and shook his head.

"They busted their buns in this drive and you just sat here and never fired your gun? Are you all right, Pa? I mean, you didn't have a seizure or a blackout or something?"

"I'm all right," Connie said. "Here."

He handed Bill his rifle.

"Did you unload it?" Bill asked

"No," Connie said.

Bill worked back the bolt-action on the ancient .30-30 and his eyes got big as an owl's.

"It's empty," he said.

"I never loaded it," Connie said.

Figures in blaze orange were emerging from the cedar swamp. They stood as their father had stood only moments before, breathing deeply, their eyes seeking their Grandpa, surveying the area around his stump, looking for a downed deer, a blood trail, *something.*

They walked slowly up the rise to Connie's stump, their eyes watching the ground all the way, seeing the deep tracks in the soft soil.

"God, Grandpa," Chuckie said, "it looks like a buffalo herd came through here. What happened? You hit any?"

"Well," Bill said quickly, "You're not gonna believe this, but this was so much fun, Grandpa wants to do this again next year."

Connie looked at the faces of his grandsons, sweaty, bewildered. Chuck had angry scratches that had drawn blood.

Connie just wanted to cry and hold them all, but that would only embarrass them. Instead, he passed around the paper cups and poured them coffee.

"Well," he said finally. "Your Dad was kidding about the next year part, I think. You know where he gets that mother wit. From his mother, of course. But, he was right about one thing . . ."

Connie took a deep slow breath, the same deep slow breath he had always taken to relax himself, to steady himself as he squeezed off the trigger on the .30-30.

"Your Dad's right about that one thing," Connie said to his grandsons. "You are not going to believe this."

Mourning

Henry Reese is one of those Wisconsin folks who lives in the city but he's the first to tell you that what he really lives for is The Deer Season.

"I dream about hunting all year long," he says. "Deer hunting! I'd rather hunt deer than anything else I can think of and probably anything else you can think of, too."

There was a time, Henry says, when, to him, "hunting" meant shooting anything that walked or ran or flew across the Wisconsin countryside. He was even crazy about bear hunting once, but when he talks about hunting today, he means going after deer and only deer.

"I went through some kind of a transition with a bear once," he admits. "There are transitions that you go through in life and in your hunting, too. Well, I went through one that just changed my hunting all around."

Henry admits that as a young man he was full of blood lust and never thought twice about the animals he killed. He remembers the time he and his brother, Gene, "walked down" a buck in the snow until its long tongue was bulging and hanging out of its mouth like a piece of liver.

"A man can walk down a deer," Henry says. "No question. That's what we did. Gene took one side of the track and I took the other, like the Indians do, and we didn't run at all, just kept up a good, steady pace so the deer could never stop to rest."

They caught up to the buck in a clearing where it was standing like a winded distance runner, plumb out of gas after a tough, pressure-packed race. The buck's chest was heaving as it tried to catch its breath and they shot it dead, a .30 caliber slug in its heart.

Henry says the only emotion he felt was elation when the buck fell. He would have taken a knife to the buck's neck if he had to, he says. He and Gene had "earned" that buck because they had walked through the same rugged country the

93

buck had, the same four-inch snow and the thick underbrush that seemed to coil in those deadly loops and snares that slashed and caught at you like barbed wire.

They had taken the buck playing by his rules. They hadn't ambushed him across a hundred yards of open valley. They hadn't run him down with dogs or a snowmobile. They hadn't used skis or snowshoes.

They had, by god, walked that deer into a state of exhaustion and their lungs and their legs had suffered the same piercing pain that his did. They had earned that buck and "earning" their buck meant "suffering" for their buck.

"I let Gene shoot it," Henry says. "Either one of us could have but at that point who fired the shot was academic because in a way we both had killed it."

"I figure it wasn't the bullet that broke that deer's heart," Henry says, "it was us."

The deer wasn't all that big and impressive, he concedes. It wasn't a trophy buck or anywhere near it.

"I mean," Henry smiles, "we're just talking your average, run-of-the-mill swamp buck that would hardly impress the good old boys over at the Legion Bar."

But Henry certainly regarded that buck as a prized specimen, a true "trophy" in its own unique way, and it had nothing to do with the number of points on the buck's head.

Hunters talk about "trophy bucks" and that didn't mean, in their estimation, that the antlers had to be a Boone & Crockett record or have 16 points or 12 or even 10. Henry thought that a trophy was exactly what Aldo Leopold had said it was.

"The trophy," Aldo Leopold wrote in his book *A Sand County Almanac*, "whether it be a bird's egg, a mess of trout, a basket of mushrooms, the photograph of a bear, the pressed specimen of a wildflower, or a note tucked into a cairn of a mountain peak, is a certificate. It attests that its owner has been somewhere and done something—that he has exercised skill, persistence and discrimination in the age-old feat of overcoming, outwitting or reducing-to-possession. These connotations which attach to the trophy usually far exceed its physical value."

That particular buck, like all the others over the years, had come out of the Star Lake/Plum Lake country around Sayner, where Henry has always hunted deer and which he loves better than any place in Wisconsin or, for that matter, the world.

It was up there in that tangled North Woods country that Henry encountered his legendary black bear and went through his "transition."

"It was back awhile," he says. "I'm not sure exactly what year it was, but it was the last deer season you could shoot a bear on a deer license."

Behind his glasses, Henry's blue eyes glitter with that excitement that hunters get whether they're in duck blinds or on deer stands or just hunkered down on a bar stool at the Legion Bar, reminiscing about being in duck blinds and on deer stands.

"I always wanted to kill a bear ever since I can remember," Henry confides. "I think it had something to do with the way bears smell. You know, you can smell a bear in the woods for miles, it seems. That distinctive smell of a bear pile makes the hair stand right up on the back of your neck and puts the fear of God in you."

Henry says it seemed as though the bear wanted you to smell him and to know that he was out there somewhere—to let that work on your mind a little.

"I'm not talking about hunting bear with an infantry company," Henry says disdainfully, "and walkie-talkies and dogs and enough fire power to invade Grenada. I'm talking about being out in the woods alone or on a deer stand alone or up-to-here in a cedar swamp, alone and smelling that bear out there. Being alone makes it a whole different ball game.

"Just you and that bear."

Henry says he was smelling bears on his deer hunts for about ten to fifteen years before he ever saw one. He and Gene smelled out not only bear piles, but the branches and tree trunks that bears had broken apart.

Bears have a "musty" smell, Henry says, and once you smell it, you never forget it.

"If you grew up on a farm," he says, "you'd swear it was kind of like an old boar in the hog pen."

One late Saturday afternoon, on a deer drive, they smelled that musty scent and it was so strong they decided to come back the next day and get serious. Deer hunting had fallen off anyway and everybody was frustrated. They hunted with the same dozen guys every year but everybody hunted independently so Gene and Henry talked the gang into organizing a drive.

"Gene and I were driving together," Henry says,"and, all of a sudden, Gene says, "There's a raccoon.' Well, it was a pretty big raccoon.

"I think Gene didn't want to see a bear, but that's what we were seeing: A bear!"

The bear galloped toward where Bob Vogel had a stand on the right and Al Trumpy had one on the left. So, no matter which way the bear went, there was a sharpshooter waiting, It turned right and Vogel nailed it through the heart with one shot—a black bear that Henry estimated weighed 300 pounds.

They gutted out the bear and left the warm intestines in a steaming pile and Henry says it's true that "the muscle structure in the bear's chest does make it look like a naked man, but that didn't bother me too much."

That wasn't the "transition." The transition came the next day.

Henry and Gene were back in the woods, looking for their trophy deer. They were sneak hunting, Henry remembers. That's where you walk, not quite together, maybe fifty, a hundred yards apart, just kind of angling through the woods, past some object or point, always in sight of each other.

Henry says they were within maybe five hundred yards of where Vogel had shot the bear the previous day when they heard a sound they had never heard before.

"It was an ungodly sound," Henry says.

Their first thought, Henry says, was that it was "the Polish guys from South Milwaukee" doing a deer drive in the vicinity. There were ten of them and they stayed up at Shorty's Hillside Tavern on County Trunk N. They had a leader called "Baldy" who carried a whistle. They also had an old second-hand police paddy wagon and they'd go from one hunting spot to another in that paddy wagon. They'd finish a deer drive, Baldy would blow a whistle and they'd all come back to the paddy wagon.

"You'd see them chuggin' all around the area," Henry says. "They'd be sitting there like soldiers in an old Army truck, guys on both sides."

On a deer drive, Henry points out, it's not uncommon for the drivers to make "crazy noises" just to get the deer alarmed and moving toward the hunters waiting on the stands.

"Some drivers," Henry smiles, "go 'toot-toot' or 'tweet-tweet' or 'bang-bang!'

"You hear goofy things and you find yourself saying goofy things. People run out of things to say. You hear them yelling: 'Ook! Aach! Bear! Bear! Deer! Deer! Move, Move! Run, Run! Flush! Flush!' I thought I even heard some of the Polish guys yelling out 'kielbasa!' a couple of times."

Henry confesses that when they first hear the "ungodly" sound, his first thought was that it was one of Baldy's boys who had too much to drink at Shorty's the night before.

"All of a sudden," Henry recalls, "that voice struck a higher note and it stopped us right in our tracks. My brother had one foot raised off the ground and I saw him just freeze there. He told me later that I was in a similar position, one foot raised and stopped dead, so that voice had the same effect on both of us."

Recovering, Henry and Gene ran toward that high-pitched voice that seemed to Henry to be almost a human in pain, and yet not human. They dashed through the heavy trees, into a clearing.

"It was the same place where Vogel had killed the bear," Henry says, "and kneeling over the guts was a sow bear, wailing. The ungodly, high-pitched voice was coming from her!

"She was raising up on her hind legs and then coming down on all four and doing all this wailing. She rose up, oh, three or four times. She was right over the spot where the bear had been killed and dressed out and I just knew that she was his mate.

"His guts were still there and you just knew she was feeling emotion. She was feeling empathy. She was mourning him!"

Even as Henry speaks, I can see that widow bear in my mind's eye and then, as though superimposed upon her, I can see the desolated, devastated faces of all the widow women I have ever known. Old women, young women, child women. They were the women of our family covered in black, all the women of the world covered in black, all the widows of dead men, wearing their black veils and clothes, crying inconsolably, wailing, screaming.

When did it start? When did the human animal first know loss and grieve? When did we first experience the pain of loss so great that it carries the human voice into another dimension, a dimension that seems not of this Earth? It is beyond crying and wailing.

The ancients called it keening—the sound of loss beyond words, beyond description, beyond telling. But, a she-bear?

"Our nephew, Danny," Henry continues, "had heard all the commotion and he came roaring out and he's quite a hunter. He had the old instinct. He wasn't soft like Gene and I were. He didn't associate it that way.

"Danny raised up his .30-30 to shoot the bear and Gene just turned the gun away. He shoved the barrel so Danny couldn't shoot and it took ten years before Danny got over that.

"While we calmed Danny down, the bear sort of faded away."

Henry understood why Danny was so upset but all of a sudden getting a bear as a trophy wasn't important to Henry or to Gene.

"Understand, we didn't feel that the bear was 'human,' " Henry says, "but we did feel a lot closer association to it than we did the day before."

Henry has never hunted bear since that day. He still hunts deer, though, and he'll be up in the Star Lake/Plum Lake country again this year, looking for that big buck, as he has since he was a boy. His hunts will take him past the spot where the bear was killed and where his mate found what was left of him.

Of course, Henry admits, should he ever hear that "ungodly wailing" again and this time it turns out to be a doe, he probably would have to rethink the whole situation.

The Season of Hunters

Winter in the North Country, Steady Eddy likes to say, just sort of sneaks up on you while you're still thinking of taking down the screens and wondering where in hell you stashed the Sorel boots last spring.

It happened again this year.

One day the little lake was still open and stuffed with so many black ducks puddling in the slush and pack ice that it looked like a rich raisin pudding out there, simmering in the steam and waiting for Christmas Eve.

Then, the very next morning, the ducks were gone, the simmering and the steam had vanished into thin, cold air, and the surface was a sheet of flat ice from shore to shore. It looked like Siberia.

The temperature plummeted, and Steady said the drop reminded him of those heavy cannonballs—"We're talking antimatter here"—off the stern of the Sheboygan charter boat *Dumper Dan*, carrying those blue-silver salmon spoons into the numbing depths of Lake Michigan.

By noon, a human being could walk on the surface of the frozen little lake, and one did, tentatively. The ice seemed rubbery, undulating underfoot. This was the thin ice that authorities warned you about. This was also the thin ice that fishermen love, and the venturesome would be out here as soon as they tested it from shore by throwing heavy branches and heavier stones onto the ice, then gauging the clunks and judging the radial cracks.

By midafternoon, a flight of Canada geese came in from the gray north skies and landed, some of them skidding and careening across the ice not so much like birds, but more like otters on a mud slide.

There was no open water, and it made you wonder why the geese bothered to land here at all, except that as Hugo Willie says over at the Gasoline Emporium: "Canada geese are just like that.

"They like to fool around," Hugo Willie says. "You talk about otters, well, Canadas sure have a lot of otter in them. Those birds just love to poke around and explore and go where no bird had gone before. Hell, as long as they've got their health, and their wing feathers aren't shot up, they'll stop right on the edge of bad weather or an ice front because they know there's always open water to the south and they can make it nonstop if they're really pushed and have to."

Geese are always wary in the North Country autumn. Autumn is the season of the hunters, and every goose coming down from Canada knows it. Steady says it gets imprinted in their brains along with their flight maps and navigation charts, which they don't get from Triple A.

"Geese don't get lost," Hugo Willie says. "They know where they are, and they know where you are."

Far out on the little lake, the geese stood around on this Sunday morning like a congregation after church is out. The wind carried their babbling and gabbling over the ice like bits of fluff, feathers. If you closed your eyes, you could convince yourself it was a pack of hounds out there, marooned on the ice and wondering where the hell the raccoons went—not to mention the trees.

Sure, these geese had been shot at. That's why they assembled in the middle of nowhere, where nothing could sneak up on them or reach them. Through the binoculars, you could see the sentinels posted, heads up, alert as cobras, while the off-duty geese gossiped like parishioners at St. Theresa's while they waited for Father Himmelsbach, who was changing from his Mass vestments into his hunting vest.

Aldo Leopold had written all about geese smarts in his book *A Sand County Almanac.*

"The geese that proclaim the seasons to our farm," Aldo had noted, "are aware of many things including the Wisconsin statutes. The south-bound November flocks pass over us high and haughty, with scarcely a honk of recognition for their favorite sandbars and sloughs. 'As a crow flies' is crooked compared with their undeviating aim at the nearest big lake twenty miles to the south, where they loaf by day on broadwaters and filch corn by night from the freshly cut stubbles. November geese are aware that every marsh and pond bristles from dawn till dark with hopeful guns."

I spent an hour, then another, watching the fat goosebirds frolicking on the frozen lake—"Frolicking?" Hugo Willie would ask later.

But, as the Indian explained it, if we were standing barefoot out there on the ice, "We'd be moving our feet plenty, too, you bet! Not to mention our tails."

I was reluctant to leave the geese because I knew that once they took off, they would go south to open water and they wouldn't be back until spring. Some of them wouldn't be back at all, because they would be shot during the winter in some other patch of water or marsh that never freezes and where even now hunters were waiting and watching the skies for fat geese coming from the north.

I watched the geese goof around for most of the afternoon. As the early dark began to come on, I started to walk along the narrow road that skirts the lake because, unlike the geese, I was not equipped to spend this night out in the open, out under the cold North Country sky.

With a great honking and hullabaloo, the geese started taking off, swinging to the south in shifting, drifting strings. The matriarch goose had made up her mind. They were going. At the very tail end, a pair swung away and flew low, directly over me. I could hear their wing beats. I said, Goodbye, Nana. Goodbye, Papa. I stood in the road and waved. A pickup truck with some hunters swerved past me. They thought I was nuts.

The Deer Hunters

Walt Goldsworthy, one of the Good Old Boys up at Three Lakes who remembers trains, drops a note to say that his letter writing has been a little slow because he came down with with what used to be called "the rheumatiz."

Once, old-timers sat around the wood stove in the depot discussing their rheumatiz and lumbago and the feared "arthur-itis," which could turn your fingers into bird's claws and your hands into plaster of Paris.

We young pups would sit by the stove thawing out from skating or sledding or icefishing, and the Old Coots would be telling us we didn't know what pain was until you got rheumatiz or lumbago or the feared "arthur-itis."

The old-timers said that if ever we got a shotgun load of rock salt in our rear ends sometime while raiding somebody's summer garden, that would give us a teeny-tiny idea of what the feared "arthur-itis" felt like. Only the pain would be not only in our little rear ends, but in every single part of our little bodies.

"In every single part?" one of the thawing young pups would always ask.

"In every single part," one of the old Coots would always reply, "where you got bone."

It left an impression on all of us. We got to calling the depot the "bone yard," but we never called it that when the Old Coots were around.

The Old Coots are all gone now, but I think of them every time I come off the trout streams these days and stick my rod hand under the hot-water tap and let the finger bones soak in temperatures hot enough to steam clams.

"My apologies for not being more prompt," Walt Goldsworthy starts out, "but we've had a rough summer. I didn't learn until early October that I was suffering from polymyalis rheumatica, a condition in which the body's immune system is fighting with the joints and muscles.

"I had credited this creeping pain and stiffness to old age—and a jolting fall I took early last spring when I climbed onto an old dead balsam log windfall that exploded without warning and pitched me forward, knocking me out for a while.

"The Three Lakes Historical Society Inc. and Museum, which is my forte as a retiree, had an exceptionally busy summer. I wear many hats there, and Doris wears two: curator and secretary-treasurer. Anyway, we enjoy it and are using God's talents until He calls us home. I have little patience for those retirees who sit and cry and pity themselves.

"Deer season opened on Saturday the 18th, and as usual Father George Votruba offered the 7 o'clock Saturday evening Deer Hunters' Mass, while across the street Pastor Ron McDuffie and his church family were busy preparing and serving up the annual Harvest Dinner. 'One of the best yet,' opined Gene Step, who, along with his bachelor buddies Dave Nelsen, Dusty Rhoades, Jim Pomas and Ray Polarski—the 'Fiddle Maker'—attested to the savory menu.

"Roast turkey, mashed potatoes, boatloads of steaming gravy, wild rice stuffing, yams, squash, apple, pumpkin and mincemeat pies and an assortment of homemade breads were all served in generous proportions.

"Meanwhile, up north at Clearwater Lake, the big attraction was the live exotic entertainment at the bar across from the old general store. Cars packed both sides of Highway 45 as the deer hunters flocked in to see the 'two-legged does' strut their stuff. Shows ran from 3 p.m. to closing the next a.m. Mae Brest—'Biggest in the West'—Nikki Knocker, Miss Nude Northwest, plus a long line of other strippers all helped add a new tagline to the deer season: 'Bucks, Beer and Breasts!'

"Truly, this is a far cry from the old days written of by Ed Epler in his last book, *Eighty Years in God's Country*, in which he tells of the time a troop of 'painted ladies' came to town one springtime to entertain the lumberjacks who were just in from a winter in the woods.

"The local women banded together and chased the new-comers out of town with sticks, brooms and bullwhips!

"Sadly, the sport of deer hunting has become badly diluted by the influx of macho-Rambo characters afield with all the paramilitary gadgets such as greasepaint, tree stands, plywood blinds, etc. Added to this 'six-pack mentality' is a lack of appreciation for Nature and the growing indifference to environmental damage and ethical ideas.

"Gene tells of checking out an old deerstand up in the Pine River country, only to find that a trail had been slashed through with a chainsaw, plywood hauled in for a blind, and several old cedar trees cut down for a better view of the ravine out front. The whole site was cluttered with empty beer cans and straw, shelled corn, a scent pit and garbage.

"The 'spiritual aspects' generated by the hunting seasons of yesteryear, when Ed Epler, Archy Nelsen, Dave Nelsen Sr. and other old-timers headed into the Sevenmile country, are rapidly fading.

"Since the public lands are a God-given heritage for all Americans to enjoy—nonhunter as well as hunter—the time is at hand for some rational thinking and planning before this generation leaves behind a generation of mutants who will never know the spiritual consolations of Nature, of the hunt and the hiking trail.

"Oh, you should come up and enjoy Christmas breakfast with Dee Koehn in the Country House Bed & Breakfast Inn at Three Lakes Haven Resort, six miles east of town at 7265 Chicken in the Woods Road. Dee is a hard worker.

"Regards. Shalom."

A Special Thanks

For a number of hunting seasons, Mary Louise and Keith Symon have permitted a small group of hunters to hunt their old farm out near Spring Green in the Wyoming Valley country that Frank Lloyd Wright made famous.

In exchange for the privilege of chasing those sleek, corn-fed whitetails up hill and dale, the grateful hunters have supplied the Symons not only with venison steaks from their successful hunts, but also with bass fillets and frozen packets of sweet morsel panfish throughout the year.

Now the hunters have sent what just might be the most wondrous gift of all.

"I don't know how you can beat a package of bluegills," Steady Eddy says, "but this comes close."

What the hunters sent to the Symons was a photocopy of what looked to be a column out of a newspaper or magazine. There was no byline. No attribution.

"Who knows," Steady Eddy speculates, "maybe one of those hunters composed it himself but just won't admit it because he doesn't want his peer group to know one of their number can write."

In any event, Steady says, this is yet another item that deserves to be posted on refrigerator doors and American Legion Bar beer coolers throughout our fair state.

"I took a walk on your land today," the unknown writer begins. "I crossed the barbwire and traversed again the familiar fields and coverts where I've often hunted in the past.

"Through the cedar tangles I walked, past the spring below the old cabin and among the aging cottonwoods and walnut trees which have guarded the draw from a thousand prairie storms. I left my tracks in the sand along the clear, narrow stream and now they are mingled with the tracks of deer and turkeys and all the wild inhabitants that depend on the water for life.

"I climbed the winding lane which leads to the hilltop and sat to rest on a stump among the brown leaves which still clung to the dormant maples. It gave me time to see the red-bellied woodpecker emerge from a hold in the dying elm on his way to an afternoon meal.

"I stood a long time on the bluff over the dry creek bed, with the wind in my face, and pondered the ridges that stretched away like waves on the ocean. The limitless sky which gathered them up in the distance only served to accentuate the feeling of space without ending.

"I chewed a handful of sumac berries to know again their eye-squinting sourness, akin to that of a fresh lemon.

"Where the fallen tree crosses the river, there was ample evidence that a raccoon was a frequent visitor to the natural bridge. The piles of spoor, rich with seeds of moonvine and grape and honey-locust would soon be swept by wind and snow into the flowing water below and some would take root downstream in another season.

"I quietly followed the deer trail which led along the base of the hill, and where the trees got smaller and thicker as the trail opens into the bluestem clearing, I saw a doe and her grownup fawns bound away from their beds.

"At the giant burr oak with the lightning scar, a great horned owl silently fled my intrusion. Maybe it was responsible for the death of the wild turkey found in the nearby pasture. I studied the signs of the feast, marked only by the checkered pinions of the once-powerful wings and I turned away, wondering.

"The air got cold as the sun dipped low and the orange-pink color for which there is no name flared gloriously against the deepening blue which sought to extinguish it. It must have stirred the coyote, for his sudden, clear high note rang from a distant ridge before trailing off with the light.

"Yes, I was on your land today. I was there because I have no place of my own to visit. I was there because you once answered 'yes' to a stranger who asked permission to hunt the wild places that belong to you. I was there because you have since given me the privilege to come and go as I wished.

"We've become good friends, you and I. I remember the winter days we spent around your fireplace, discussing whether a big cat really lives on your river, and the summer hours swapping stories while fixing your fence. I remember the morning you invited me in, half-frozen, for a hot piece of pie that I'm sure was intended for dinner's company. And the time we walked together on your land, when I learned by watching and listening just how you felt about it.

"I have offered little in return for your generosity—a bird now and then or a mess of fish. But I want you to know that the access you freely give, whether it be on five acres or a thousand, means a lot to me, and in many ways, I feel the same about your land as you do.

"So, I wanted to share what I saw today, that you might realize that what you own is not just a place to hunt, but a special tie to something everyone wishes that he had.

"I thank you on behalf of all the hunters and fishermen who have learned that an outdoor experience goes beyond setting a hook or pulling a trigger—that it reaches further than open season or legal limits—that it increases our awareness of ourselves and the world around us.

"It is on your home ground that many of us have tasted the land and the freedom it offers. And we are grateful."

Steady says THAT beats a thank-you from Hallmark.

Wisdom from Animals

What is it about wild geese that raises not only our eyes but also our spirits to the skies?

Mel Ellis, one of Wisconsin's most beloved outdoor writers, felt that humans identified with wild geese because wild geese embody the traits that we landbound ones hold so dear: Love of *freedom*. Love of *family*. Love of *adventure*.

Mel so identified with the great Canada geese that he called one of his books *Wild Goose, Brother Goose*. That cost him an editorship at a leading outdoor magazine because his bosses decided he was "too anthropomorphic."

"A March morning," Aldo Leopold wrote in *A Sand County Almanac*—and he could have been writing about Mel's bosses at the magazine—"is only as drab as he who walks in it without a glance skyward, ear cocked for geese. I once knew an educated lady, banded by Phi Beta Kappa, who told me that she had never heard or seen the geese that twice a year proclaim the revolving seasons to her well-insulated roof. Is education possibly a process of trading awareness for things of lesser worth? The goose who trades his is soon a pile of feathers."

Like Mel Ellis and Aldo Leopold, Pastor Andrew Rogness of Advent Lutheran Church down in Madison is not ashamed to admit that his flock includes the wild geese and that he is a brother to them, too.

Pastor Rogness, who is torn these days between putting away his cross-country skis and hauling out his canoe, has sent along a note that will just get your spirits up and honking.

"I'm enclosing a little piece from my synod newsletter," Pastor Rogness writes. "Nice to know that others in my church seek wisdom from animals."

The little piece he enclosed is called "A Lesson from the Geese," credited to Milton Olson. It appeared in the March 1988 edition of the *Nebraska Synod Update.*

Milton Olson lists five lessons that the wild geese teach us. Steady Eddy says that Milton and Mel are birds of a feather.

"Number One," Milton begins his list, "as each bird flaps its wings, it creates an uplift for the bird following. By flying in a V formation, the whole flock adds 71-percent more flying range than if each bird flew alone.

"*Lesson: People who share a common direction and sense of community can get where they are going quicker and easier because they are traveling on the thrust of one another.*

"Number Two," Milton says. "Whenever a goose falls out of formation, it suddenly feels the drag and resistance of trying to fly alone and quickly gets back into formation to take advantage of the 'lifting power' of the bird immediately in front.

"*Lesson: If we have as much sense as a goose, we will stay in formation with those headed where we want to go.*

"Number Three," Milton continues. "When the lead goose gets tired, it rotates back into the formation and another goose flies at the point position.

"*Lesson: It pays to take turns doing the hard tasks and sharing leadership with people as with geese—interdependent on each other.*

"Number Four," Milton says. "These geese in formation honk from behind to encourage those up front to keep up their speed.

"*Lesson: We need to make sure our honking from behind is encouraging—not something less helpful.*

"Number Five," Milton concludes. "When a goose gets sick or shot down, two geese drop out of formation to follow him down to help and protect him. They stay with him until he is either able to fly again or dies. Then they launch out with another formation to catch up with their flock.

"Lesson: If we have as much sense as the geese, we'll stand by each other like that."

Steady Eddy thinks that one of the things that humans admire about Canada geese is their faithfulness. They do indeed stand by each other. Canada geese mate for life.

"Canadas aren't into one-night stands," Steady says. "We're talking commitment here and I think that appeals to all of us in our secret hearts. I mean, Canadas are really in for the duration. I think humans would like to be."

Aldo Leopold noted that in watching the daily routines of a spring goose convention in the corn stubbles, he noticed that prevalence of singles—lone geese that do much flying about and much talking. One could impute a disconsolate tone to their honkings and jump to the conclusion that they were broken-hearted widowers or mothers hunting lost children.

"The seasoned ornithologist," Aldo commented, "knows, however, that such subjective interpretation of bird behavior is risky."

Aldo reported that after he and his students had spent a half-dozen years counting geese in a flock, unexpected light was shed on the meaning of "lone geese." By mathematical analysis, Aldo's students found that flocks of six or multiples of six were far more frequent than chance alone would dictate.

"In other words," Aldo Leopold summed up, "goose flocks are families or aggregations of families, and lone geese in the spring are probably what our fond imaginings had first suggested. They are the bereaved survivors of the winter's shooting, searching in vain for their kin. Now, I am free to grieve with, and for, the lone honkers."

"I dunno," Steady says. "Ain't that *anthropomorphic?*"

WINTER

On Big Pond

We went out to the professor's coulee country farm last Sunday to prune the black bass population in the frozen Big Pond.

The prof said that as far as he knew, it was the first time that anybody had fished that pond in the winter since he had it built in the valley bottom to help Ma Nature out a little.

Initially, the prof had planted rainbow trout in the pond. They provided a couple of carnival seasons and then they just petered out and were gone.

"The locals seem to smell out trout," the prof said, "and this valley is kind of remote and isolated. But I don't think the pond got poached all that much. Oh sure, a few trout here and there. But nobody fished them to extinction."

Still, if poachers hadn't taken all the trout, who or what had? Because sure as God made little hand-tied woolly nymphs, the fat and sassy rainbow trout were all gone.

"They grew about an inch a month for the 18 months they were in the pond," the prof said. "I don't think they starved to death."

The plot thickened. If it wasn't poachers and it wasn't the pantry, what was it?

111

The prof said his son and some friends had combed the pond on a whole series of trout-finding scuba dives and they hadn't found a single rainbow, alive or dead.

One of the prof's fish biologist friends tested the water and the food supply and watched the outflow through the culvert in the manmade earthen dam.

At one time or another, he had a thermometer at every foot of the pond's 10-foot depth until he finally knew as much about that water as any fish that ever lived in it.

One memorable day, with his data sheets in one hand and a bottle of beer in the other, the prof's friend concluded that the pond was just about ideal for trout except for one little thing: The pond didn't have enough oxygen for trout. That will kill them every time.

His professional recommendation was "to stop playing God and just stock some nice ordinary largemouth black bass in here like any halfway smart person would. And DON'T put any bluegills in here with them!"

The prof hated to give up his dream of a trout fishery in that magic valley, but the prof is a realist first and a dreamer second, so he listened to his biologist friend and stocked the pond with largemouth bass.

The bass thrived and reproduced, something the rainbows had never done.

"The rainbows were a real put-and-take fishery," the prof says. "I put and Nature took. I would have been money ahead fishing at Kohl's supermarket."

The black bass multiplied so well that the prof had to organize regular expeditions of his friends to come in to the valley fishery and "prune back" the bass population. The little fish were taxing the limited food supply in the pond and threatening to stunt the growth of the whole tribe.

As I drilled out the very first hole, the prof's son told me about the time they had gone to see their Norwegian cousins up at their pond in the winter—and somebody got the bright idea of chopping out a big rectangle in the ice into which they inserted their rowboat, climbed in, and sat there ice fishing. He said they had a picture somewhere.

I looked at him closely, because the son is a chip off the old Nordic block and can keep a straight face in the most outlandish circumstances. He likes to test anyone over 30 for senility.

It was work for the halcyon days of summer—serious, scientific work with observations of lengths and weights and age classes. Field study was followed by the even more serious work of filleting the seminar bass, frying them up in the Paul Bunyan pan (as big and heavy as a wagon wheel, a candidate for weight rooms throughout the National Football League), and washing down the crinkly bass morsels with glaciated bottles of beer that had been soaking in the spring house, wherein the waters are clear as gin and every bit as numbing.

"We didn't want them to spoil, you know," Steady Eddy says.

"We never fished the bass in the wintertime," the prof says, "because I just assumed that they went into hibernation until spring."

"Naturally," Steady Eddy says, "you would think they would be as comatose as any other self-respecting denizen of Wisconsin in the wintertime. Comatose goes with the territory. What always held me back on fishing black bass in the frozen wastes was the difficulty of casting a lure into that little bitty hole in the ice."

The prof, the prof's son, and I sat out there on Big Pond for a spell and we got zero fish. Within the hour, they decided they'd walk back to the house and hunt grouse along the way. I could bring the four-wheel drive up when I came back.

When I packed it in, I had six bass in the pail and I had heard six shots popping in the hills. They had seen "maybe fifteen" grouse and the son had shot two.

It was early when we headed home—before 6 o'clock— but winter dark. On the Big Pond, the bass holes were skimming over and freezing shut.

Warm Memories

T*he crows are coming to clean our woods.*
     Beneath their wings, a littered world waits.
The snowfield like some frozen surf
Releases dead things to the sun.

Little bodies and bits of fur
Dead, these fifty days and more.
The old French called it Butte des Morts
Hill of the Dead.
We mourn them too.

There was a thaw last week. February 22 looked like March 22. There was water everywhere, tinkling and plopping into pools and ponds, running down the oaks, darkening the ancient bark with wetness, releasing the damp musk of soil, and fermenting detritus so pungent and pregnant with promises of days to come.

With the thaw came a remembrance of days past. February 22 is Grandpa's birthday. I lit a candle for him, opened the Dutch door and just hung out with the Old Country Man for a while. He's been dead now for a lifetime.

I got left with my grandparents a lot when I was very, very young. I thought later that it must have had something to do with Prohibition. My folks stashed me at my mother's folks' for safekeeping while they, like everyone else in town, took on the federal government agents who always seemed to come on their raids wearing overcoats no matter what the weather. According to the "old country" people, the agents couldn't be reasoned with because none of them seemed to be drinkers.

That wasn't true of Pinky, the motorcycle cop who was a member of the South Milwaukee Police Department. There was also a man named Wink in the department, and I remember Tata laughing about them: "Pinky, Winky," he would say. I think that for the longest time, those were the only two words in English that he knew.

Pinky would roar up to the tiny frame house on a big white Harley in his boots and jacket. His goggles would be down, like he was on official police business. Then he'd park the bike and come into the kitchen.

The most prominent thing about Pinky was his red face, The coloring was partly due to sunburn and windburn and—if it isn't too unkind to say so—partly due to his intake of spirits, some of which he always sampled when he stopped in to visit Tata and Baba.

"Baba!" Pinky would greet Grandma, and Grandpa would pour him a glass of home-brewed wine.

Grandpa made the wine in huge crocks, and I seem to remember that Pinky didn't really mind if the wine hadn't finished fermenting. He would dip his glass into the crock, scooping up the wine, skins and all. (Perhaps that's only my imagination working now as the grapes worked then.)

I think Pinky was really as gentle as my Grandpa, and I think he stopped not only for the wine, but for the haltingly voiced sociability and the chickens and the geese and the magnificent German shepherd that Grandpa named Nellie.

Tata had trained the dog so well that she would never touch or harass the chickens, geese, or cats. She kept me from wandering into trouble by clamping her jaws over my wrist and persuading me to stay out of harm's way. Tata said he was particularly proud of the fact that while this was going on, I could be pulling her hair or hitting her and *never once* did Nellie lose her composure, not to mention her temper.

Pinky could pat her, and that always struck us as funny: *A police dog with a policeman.* As Steady Eddy says, we were all innocents back then.

I remember only two great traumatic times from those days. One was when Grandpa and I were out in the woods picking mushrooms. He slumped down to the ground and got pale and cold; I thought he was dead. I ran all the way home and told Baba; she got help and they came and carried Grandpa home.

They said it was a stroke from the heat, but we were in a shady woods. I don't know what it was because they never told me. One of the first things Grandpa said when he came to was: Did we bring the mushrooms? I think somebody had.

The other great time of trauma was when Nellie disappeared. Grandpa and Grandma always said that somebody must have stolen her against her will because she never, ever strayed. It was like the "heat stroke"; they weren't telling everything they knew.

It's possible that she had gone into heat and left because no dogs came around, but, as Steady says, that's kind of unusual.

"Dogs can surround your house," Steady says, "quicker than a first mortgage. We're talking radar."

Nellie was gone for weeks and weeks, and then one day she just came back. But she was different.

Her pads were worn, as though she had traveled a long way. She snapped and snarled at Grandpa and wouldn't eat or drink. Grandpa told Grandma that he thought Nellie had been poisoned. You couldn't pet her or get close to her, and I don't remember trying. I don't exactly recall what happened, but Grandpa said later that she had been attacking me and that he had called Pinky.

Grandpa shooed me away and talked to Pinky, and they were both trying to talk to Nellie, and Nellie was growling and snarling, and then there was an explosion, a gunshot, and the next thing I remember was that they were putting Nellie in the back of a truck. Her bowels had emptied and I cried like a baby. Grandpa was crying too, and so was Pinky. Baba hugged me and the truck drove away.

After that, nothing really bad happened for years and years and years.

Gales of November

A couple of golden autumnal days up at the Kellman cabin in Door County always has a salutary effect on me.

What happens on those sweeping Lake Michigan beaches is cleansing. It just airs you out like laundry on the line.

Steady Eddy insists it's the view. Up here, you can sit in an outdoor john with the door wide open and just stare out at the vastness of Lake Michigan. "And you can do that," Steady says, "for hours on end."

Only the herring gulls and God know you're there.

You could be back in the 1800's. It's a trip.

"I'm serious," Steady Eddy says. "They should start putting in outdoor johns for the tourists up here and they can forget about miniature golf and the waterslides."

There are places in the North Country where you go primarily to fish or hunt or canoe or whatever. I know folks who drive out of their way just to watch an icefishing practice in the beer cooler at the Legion Bar in Three Lakes.

The Kellman cottage is a place where you go primarily to beachcomb. Oh, you say that you're just going to walk the beach up to the Sturgeon Bay Ship Canal and back, but what you're really going to do is beachcomb. Particularly after a big storm, and autumn is the season of the big storms on the Great Lakes.

When you prowl these beaches after a storm, it's easy to slip back into another time when you were a boy on the Point Beach outside of Two Rivers, picking and poking through the aftermath of a storm. I LOVE the storms in this season. Steady says sure, that's because we're safely on shore, playing cribbage with a dry deck. He's right. I even love sitting through storms with the john door open and thinking of old John Muir, riding out a California rainstorm high in the branches of a tree, just howling like a wolf with happiness.

I walked the beach after our most recent storm. Tangles of seaweed were piled high upon the sands, marking the true boundaries of this lake. The tangles were cylindrical, rolled-up universes containing dead alewives and dead beer cans and miles of balled-up monofilament compressed into a ganglia, lifeless as guts pulled from fish.

In the sea wrack lies a green, jointed J Plug, disgorged by the lake, returned to the world of man. The lake is like some great animal, picking, licking its body, digesting everything it can and spitting out everythng it cannot.

Down the beach, south of Kellman's cottage, a neighbor from out-of-state who is never here when we are has worked diligently over the seasons to build a permanent ramp for his tin fishing boat.

The ramp was made of evenly spaced, bolted-down, rein-forced concrete slabs. On a blue bright morning in another October, I cleaned a six-pound brown trout on the neighbor's permanent ramp. The herring gulls found me before I finished and I shared the fish with them.

"If the gulls had given you the guts," Steady asks, "would you have called that 'sharing?' "

When I washed the fishblood off the concrete slab, it felt as strong—and permanent—as rock. Heavy, heavy duty. Over the years, this tough, man-made structure had weathered like the great rocks offshore, its surface worn smooth in the endless ebb and flow of the waters. I even told myself that the great inland sea had "accepted" the ramp as part of itself. Steady says, "That's the Walt Disney in you."

Now, the concrete ramp was unrecognizable. The slabs that only last season seemed set here for eternity had been ripped away like boards off a barn. The slabs were visible in the shallows, strewn this way and that, looking like a load of barnboards that had slipped off the truck. It looked like the ramp had been blown apart with explosives.

The tin fishing boat was stored for the winter up near the neighbor's cabin. It sat there—"like a fish out of water," Steady says—and you got the feeling that it would be sitting there for a while while its owner sat in Illinois and figured.

On a bright, blue day it is easy to fool yourself as you look out over the calm surface of Lake Michigan and think that you are the master of all you survey. I think it's the word "lake" that fools you. *This water is not a lake.*

I remember the North Atlantic on a troopship in a winter storm and I remember this very Lake Michigan miles and miles out on an ore carrier in a November storm. This Lake Michigan was scarier. The ore boat was twice as big as the troopship but it was no contest. There are old sailors around who have sailed both saltwater and the Great Lakes and they'll tell you there wasn't enough money in the world to keep them sailing here after October ended and November came from Canada.

Everyone who hangs around the inland seas has a story for you about their awesome power: rudders torn away from the biggest carriers. Seawalls and concrete ramps blown apart. Land masses cannonaded and cascading into the angry waters like disintegrating glaciers.

My story is from a primitive little island in Lake Michigan: limestone cliffs, cobblestone beaches. No people.

We waded out below a limestone cliff and there in the motionless water lay an endless length of anchor chain, curled, black, *monstrous*. It seemed a dead sea serpent.

Each link was wider than a man. The chain must have come from an enormous ship. How many men would it take to carry this length of chain? A hundred? How much machinery to lift it? How much power? *What kind of sea was running to sweep this chain inshore like a string?*

The chain is there yet. Every time I see it, I get a funny feeling. *What kind of a sea was running that day?*

"It was salutary," Steady says. "It will clean your sinuses. It will empty your bowels. It will blow your mind."

NORTH COUNTRY
CHRISTMAS

Lip Service

They were sitting around in the American Legion Bar up in
Three Lakes the other night—"just anchoring the bar so
it doesn't drift away" is the way Steady Eddy put it—and they
got around to discussing how commercial the whole Christmas
season has gotten over the years.

"Well, you know," Gene the bartender said, "I do think
it has gotten worse since everybody got color TV. You see all
this stuff on TV and it's pretty tempting. In the old days when
there was only radio, you couldn't see all the stuff, so you had
to go downtown and window-shop. When downtown was one
street long with five stores on each side, there wasn't much of
a selection when it came to temptation. Of course, I say this
knowing full well that what is temptation for one person can
be sheer boredom to another. Dry flyfishing for example. Or
polka dancing."

Gene waited for a reaction from his customers, all two of
them: the good priest Himmelsbach and the good doctor.

"Personally speaking," Doc said, "that's exactly the kind
of loose talk I would expect from a man who has been known

to fish trout with a gob of angleworms that outweighed the trout by many pounds. In fact, may I suggest that one would be further ahead in the game if one simply fried up the bait and forsook the fishing altogether. Having eaten crow on other fishless occasions, 'tis but a short stop to eating worms."

"Aaah," Father Himmelsbach intoned in that voice he can bounce off the back wall of St. Theresa's like a tennis ball, "it would seem that we are full of the Christmas spirit here."

"We're full of something," Gene said.

" 'Nobody loves me,' " Doc sang out, " 'everybody hates me. Might as well go eat worms.' Did you ever sing that when you were little?"

"When I was little," Father Himmelsbach said, "we had a nun who would sing that when she was trying to jolly us out of the melancholia—depression, you would call it now—that was usually brought on by a D or an F on some test. She would do this jollying in front of the whole class. I remember one boy in particular—Mike was his name. He wore his jet black hair like a Navajo. As a matter of fact, I think his father was Indian— Native American. Mike would be so sad and so glum you could cry for him. He just got so impassive he might have turned to stone. His lower lip would come straight out and he would just stand there, or sit there if he was at his desk, and I don't think you could have moved him with a team of horses or a tractor.

" 'Mike,' " Sister would say, " 'I could hang a pail on that lower lip.' Everybody in the whole class would laugh and giggle except Mike. He just seemed far away, and we used to wonder where he went to when Sister started on him. Most of the other kids never ever got sullen and did that. They either got tears in their eyes or they tried hard not to."

"Or they got A's and B's," Doc said softly.

"Or they got A's and B's," Father Himmelsbach said. "Now that I think about Mike, I don't remember him saying two words in that whole class."

"He never spoke in school?" Doc asked. "You never heard his voice?"

"I remember his voice," Father Himmelsbach said, "as mostly grunts and almost growls in class. He was very nonverbal there. But he had a very, very deep bass voice. Like a man's. A grown man's voice. There was a nun in charge of the boys'

122

choir—I think it was Sister Clementella—and I don't know how she got him to open his mouth, but she did and she got him into that choir like a shot. He was our whole bass section.

"We're talking fifth- and sixth-grade boys here and, you know, we all sounded like a bunch of canaries in a pet shop. Sister Clementella always said that we were the tinkling little silver bells and Mike was the big barrel organ. He sounded like your father up there in the choir loft. She said we were her peepers and Mike was her bullfrog. I think he liked that because in all the hours and hours of practice, especially for midnight Mass on Christmas, you never once saw Mike's lip stick out so you could hang a pail on it.

"He was just a natural. I don't know if he could read music—most of us couldn't—but Sister Clementella would sing the parts for us and it just stuck. When she sang the bass part and Mike joined in, they even looked like a couple of frogs. They hit lower and lower notes and their eyes would bulge and it seemed like the whole choir loft got to vibrating. We would all laugh and Mike would laugh too—and then Sister would remind us not to laugh when we sang at Mass.

"Midnight Mass was the first time the congregation ever heard us. The choir loft was at the back of the church, and we could look down and see everybody facing the front, wearing their Christmas finery. The sanctuary was aglow with candles, the pine smell from the manger scene filled the church, and we sang in Latin—the birds and the bullfrog sang in Latin.

"When they heard Mike, first one head turned, then another and another. By the time Communion came around, they were all turned looking up, unbelieving, as they watched us sing. As they heard Mike.

"Sister Clementella, who was standing and facing us in her Christmas starched cowl, smiled at all of us. Then she looked directly at Mike— and *her* lip came out so far, you could have hung a pail on it."

Body Heat

When you live up in the North Country in winter, you just naturally keep track of things because you could wind up freezing your buns if you don't.

So you come to know when the ice on the lakes is strong enough to support you without a snowmobile, then with a snowmobile and then, eventually, with the whole snowmobile club.

Three Lakes is just full of folks who keep track of such things. They know when certain things are supposed to happen, and if those things don't happen on schedule, they get antsy.

Well, the lakes froze over pretty much on schedule, but the Christmas creche over at St. Theresa's that's usually set up by this time wasn't,

The other night Gene and Doc were sitting in the Legion Bar having "a toddy for the body," as Doc says, when Father Himmelsbach came in, looking, as Gene says, "like a rabbit that just found out that beagles aren't family."

Gene got out the brandy, poured a shot and asked what was wrong. Father Himmelsbach knocked back the brandy.

"I can't find Jesus," he said.

"God," Doc said. "That's like your pilot telling you he can't find O'Hare."

"The Baby Jesus got lost," Father Himmelsbach said. "That's why the creche isn't up. I've been looking for a week."

"You have to ask St. Anthony," Doc said. "If St. Anthony can't find Jesus then we're all in trouble."

"Everybody else is there," Father Himmelsbach said. "Mary, Joseph, the shepherds, the three kings, the animals, the camels. Even the manger is there, but the baby Jesus is missing."

"Listen," Gene said. "We'll lock up here and go have a look-see."

"Sure," Doc said. "What could we lose?"

Father Himmelsbach didn't think that was too funny.

✿ ✿ ✿

The church was warm and cozy, the heat clunking through the pipes like little animals scuttling in the darkness. Father Himmelsbach turned on the sanctuary lights and there it was: the stable at Bethlehem. It was a disaster area. Beneath the blue spruce branches, the carved wooden figures were scattered about, the boxes and tissue paper looked like windblown debris.

Doc offered his professional opinion.

"You could say it was vandals," he said.

Gene began lining up the figures in the traditional arrangement, two lines radiating outward from the stable, with the manger in the center.

"Yeah," Doc said. "You notice right away that the crib is empty."

Gene backed up and stood there, arms akimbo. He began tapping his lips with the forefinger of his right hand. He does the same thing before he climbs into a trout stream, too.

"I just looked everywhere," Father Himmelsbach said. "You can't replace pieces like that anymore. You need an old-time carver."

"The last time I was in a sanctuary," Doc said, "I was getting married. And before that, I was serving Mass. In the old days, when it was all Latin, before they turned you guys around."

"We could skip the whole thing," Father Himmelsbach said, "but there would be hell to pay. Another tradition shot. A guitar Mass for the old-timers."

Gene was as wooden as the figures he was staring at.

"It's like riding a bicycle," Doc said. "Once you learn, you never forget. *Confiteor Deo omnipotente, beate Mariae semper virgini, beate Michaeli, archangelo, beate Johani Baptistae, sanctos apostolis, Petro et Paulo.* It's amazing how you get imprinted. I haven't said a Latin prayer since I was a little boy and there it is: I confess to almighty God, to blessed Mary, ever virgin, to blessed Michael the archangel, to blessed John the Baptist, to the holy apostles, Peter and Paul. The best part was *Mea culpa, mea culpa, mea maxima culpa.* Through my fault, through my fault, through my most grievous fault. Good time to try that one, Father."

Gene suddenly clapped his hands together, and it sounded like a pistol shot in the empty church. He leaped to the creche and began moving the wooden figures.

"We're talking about a cold night," he said. "Right? The night wind and the chill and the drafts? And a newborn baby in a stable. Now, who in his right mind is not gonna be concerned for that kid in the cold? These are folks who know all about cold nights and heat loss. We're talking survivors here. We're talking *body heat.*"

Gene moved the figures gently, nudging them to make room for the others, bunching them in tightly.

"You wrap the baby up so you don't see anything sticking out," Gene said. "You insulate him. Pile straw around him. You get his mom right over him and you get the sheep and the donkeys right up close—they're radiating heat like Coleman stoves!

"Then, you get one row of shepherds up close and behind them another row and another. You got a windbreak that won't quit. All you can see from out here is their backs. But you *know* a baby is in there. You take it on faith."

That's the way it is this Christmas in Three Lakes. Everybody crowding in, keeping the cold world off the Little One. When you think about it, that's the way it should be down here on the planet.

Church of the Holy Beer Cooler

They were sitting around at the American Legion Bar up in Three Lakes the other night, and they got to discussing the crisis that popped up during the last icefishing practice session in the beer cooler.

Some of the old traditionalists, who just like to sit there on their beer kegs zipping and unzipping their snowmobile suits and being contemplative as the Buddha, were very upset by one of the Young Turks who had the audacity to bring a tape recorder into the cooler and was playing Christmas carols for the meditating assemblage.

It had shocked the traditionalists right out of their Sorel boots, and they proceeded to hold a rump session of the membership right then and there—"on their rumps," as Steady Eddy puts it—to decide whether or not the offender should be permitted to practice in the beer cooler at all anymore. The old-timers felt strongly that the deviant young pups should be banished from the beer cooler forever, and for all they cared, he could go practice on Main Street over an open manhole.

"Well, you know," Gene the bartender was saying, "the old guys are really steamed over this. I mean, in all the years of icefishing practice in the beer cooler, not once has anybody been what you would call noisy or disturbed the peace in there. I remember in the Old Days, you couldn't get in there it was so full. I mean, it looked like Sucker Creek when the walleyes are spawning, and yet the crowd in there was as quiet and numbed as chinooks in the fish box. It was like early Mass over at St. Theresa's for the six faithful *babushkas* and that one desperate fly fisherman who every now and again asks good old God for the advice that even Trout Unlimited doesn't seem to have in the membership.

"A thing like this has to be nipped in the bud or you could have a full-fledged revolution on your hands here. You start letting tape recorders in, then next it will be radios and boomboxes and then, God forbid, television! You're not supposed to be sitting in there in the beer cooler watching television. You're supposed to be sitting out here *at the bar* watching television! We're talking tradition here. It's like church. Certain things are sacred, damn it!"

Gene waited for a reaction from his customers.

"Your impassioned argument," Doc began, "that the Legion beer cooler is as sacred as our good friend's church is an interesting observation to say the least. In view of the fact that he is the only one present intimately acquainted with both precincts, I shall defer to his expertise on the matter and will expect him to now assemble his thoughts, not to mention his wits, and fully blister your blasphemous hide for such sacrilege. In the old days, sire, only a pilgrimage, barefoot through the snows of winter, would have been proper punishment for a mouth like yours. But let us give the papal field rep that moment to check with the home office before he responds.

"Now, then, as one who has long advocated progress in the way this Legion post—dare I say outpost?—conducts its affairs, may I say that I vigorously support the actions of the young man who brought his tape recorder into the beer cooler and turned everybody off when he turned it on. Fie on the old fuddy-duddies! Fie, sir! Fie!

"By your own account, he was playing Christmas carols. Christmas carols! Is this not the Christmas season? To everything there is a season, as the good padre has told us so often that it's enough to give you a headache. Actually, more than enough. A time to play Christmas carols and a time not to play Christmas carols . . . "

Gene's eyes rolled like Cookie Monster's. Father Himmelsbach cleared his throat.

"I think," Father Himmelsbach said, "the Legion is facing what the Church has faced. New ideas. New people. Young people. Well, we dropped the Latin. And if you can turn the priest around, you can turn the world around. I think if the pope was running the beer cooler, he would compromise and let the young man bring the music in with a Walkman until the old men got used to it. Establish the beachhead. Get a toehold."

"Could he do it in your church?" Gene asked.

"We allow hearing aids." Father Himmersbach said. "I think I would look the other way."

"If you look the other way," Gene said, "you'll see Doc with a boom-box."

"No," the priest said. "Doc brings his fly box."

Gene went to fetch the eggnog that made them so funny.

The Spooky Spirit of Christmas Eve

The night before Christmas has a magic that no other night has—with the exception, Steady Eddy says, of those late witching hours on the trout streams of summer when the mayflies are hatching and the trout are beginning to roll like Harbor seals.

There is a great feeling of expectancy in the air. Something strange, something out of the ordinary is about to happen. It's a very joyous time in one sense, because Christmas means vacation from school, presents, food and cookies—and watching the uncles drink plum wine and apricot brandy on Christmas Day after the goose dinner. As a matter of fact, *before* the goose dinner, too. It's out of the ordinary because the family only does this once a year.

The strange part is the part that you really can't see.

You know the feeling? Going from room to room and all the lights are on and you expect to meet someone or see someone and all you ever meet is silence and all you ever see is just the room.

It happens only during the Christmas season, never in the summer or spring or fall. It's a *spooky* feeling. I think it's much spookier that Halloween. Most people, when you mention spooks or ghosts, think of Halloween. I always think of Christmas. The *night before Christmas.*

When we were kids, we were expecting Santa Claus, but that's not the spooky I mean. Besides, we weren't kids very long because the same big kids who told us about the birds and the bees also told us about Santa Claus.

I remember finding presents from Santa in my parents' closet a week before Christmas and I felt so guilty I told Father Kohler about it in confession and he said it wasn't a sin.

Charlie Kaiser not only found Christmas presents in his folks' closet, he opened presents and then rewrapped them. He said he never even mentioned that in confession, because he didn't feel guilty at all about it. He was just going to look surprised on Christmas morning and go on about what a wonderful man Santa was.

His folks weren't so dumb, though. Charlie's surprise on Christmas morning was genuine because they had switched presents on him, and the whole family howled about it. You could see where Charlie got his sense of humor.

The funny thing is that after we found out about Santa Claus and didn't expect him anymore, the mystery only deepened. A sort of hush, an eerie quiet set in about midafternoon on Christmas Eve, and it didn't really matter where you were at the time.

You could be in the piney woods on snowshoes and it would just come to you that you should be very watchful because you might see something unusual before you got back to the cabin. You would start looking for something in the trees. Then, you would swear that there was *something* just out of sight and it was aware of you even as you were aware of it, whatever it was.

Most people, like those who frequent the American Legion Bar in Three Lakes, scoff at that and suggest that you have had either too much brandy or not enough. The good Father Himmelsbach often came to our defense, noting that the original tenants of these forests—"who had no brandy until we came"—also felt that there was something out there. The Native Americans called it *Wendigo,* a spirit that haunted the forests, spooky and silent as ravens when the ghost shows shrouded their land. Bless you, Father.

But, the spirit of Christmas Eve is not the Wendigo because the Wendigo happens only outside in the big woods while the spooky spirit of Christmas Eve is outside and inside and *everywhere.* You can be on a Nicolet ski trail or on a fogbound Door County beach or in your own house or cabin or condo and that *something* creeps up on you and you just *know* that it is real, that it exists even as you do.

I think folks were more open about this in the olden days. The old-timey Christmas literature is full of ghosts and spirits and spooky things going bump in the dark, spooky things that whisper of a strange country away from the warmth of the Christmas kitchen.

You can get arguments from people about what it is we're celebrating on Christmas. Some folks say that we're really continuing a good pagan tradition that started out making the winter solstice when the pickings were lean. The tribal elders knew that as the rations got shorter, the days would get longer, and if the populace could be encouraged to ingest some fermented stuff, it would help the winter pass 'more quickly. That still works at The Legion.

Some folks say that the 25th of December is not the birthday of Jesus Christ. It was another day. Other folks say that no day is the birthday of Jesus Christ because Jesus Christ is a myth.

"Whatever," Steady Eddy says. "You got all these Christians celebrating a Jewish birthday and that's a miracle by itself."

In the wee hours of Christmas morning, all the grown children, travel weary and home for the holidays, are asleep in the rooms of their childhood. In the living room, the mate with whom you have decorated a forest of pagan trees puts on the last of the ornaments the children left for you to hang. The colored lights wink, blink, reflect in the window glass. Outside in the magical winter woods, something is stirring, padding in the quiet snow, approaching. It is spooky. But it is not scary.